The Power of Baked Alaska

by

Steve J Smith

The Power of Baked Alaska

Simple ways to lead people and build business

Matthew Chapter Five, Verse Thirteen:

"Ye are the salt of the earth".

1. A person or group considered as embodying simplicity and moral integrity.
2. Archaic. A person or group considered the best or most worthy part of society.

Salt of the earth—*The Free Dictionary*

THEMES

FOREWORD

When I met Steve, our relationship was one in which I was his career coach.

After he invited me to review his book and pen a foreword, I readily agreed to do so. My fifty-year career in human resource (HR) management and associated HR activities qualified me to comment on peoples' personal qualities, professional skills and career experience... the three things at the heart of Steve's book.

When we first talked, I was struck by Steve's energy, commitment, and capacity to be self-effacing: a characteristic in ample supply throughout this uniquely informative and entertaining romp through his career.

He draws on his personal career experiences with acute honesty and provides a plethora of anecdotes on leadership, sales, promotions and their resulting successes and failures; all of which make this book a most unusual and welcome contribution to the crowded (some would say, overcrowded) market for business books.

Steve admits to having had as many downs as ups, but through it all comes bright lights of wisdom and humour, in equal measure.

I heartily recommend *Baked Alaska,* especially for those of us who have grown weary of the over full bookshelves of self-important tomes! This is the authentic, real deal.

Colin Parry OBE, JP, FCIPD

CHRONOLOGY

Born in St. Helens

Nutgrove Primary, Grange Park High School

Widnes Sixth Form College

University of Sheffield

Procter & Gamble

The Kellogg Company

AG Barr plc

Business Doctors

KEY TERMS

Blue-Chip: Companies with stable and strong financial track records based on continuous success

Brand: Product manufactured by a particular company, under a particular name

CEO: Chief Executive Officer

Consumers: The end users of a product

Customers: The purchaser of products, usually a wholesaler or retailer for onward selling

FMCG   Fast moving consumer goods

HBR   Harvard Business Review

HR   Human Resources (Personnel)

MD   Managing Director

Multiples: Grocery chains who buy direct from suppliers (e.g., Asda, Co-operative, Tesco)

NPD: New Product Development

PA: Personal Assistant

PLC: Public Limited Company

Shopper: The person who buys the product in-store, but may not be the actual consumer of it

SKU: Shelf (or Stock) Keeping Unit (e.g. 500g packet of Cornflakes is one SKU

SME: Small to Medium sized Enterprise

Wholesalers: 'Middlemen' who buy in bulk from suppliers and sell to small retailers (e.g., Booker)

USP: Unique Selling Proposition of a product

SCENE SETTING

FMCG or consumer packaged goods are products that are sold quickly at a relatively low cost. Examples include non-durable household goods such as packaged foods, beverages, toiletries, over-the-counter medicines and other consumable products. Wholesalers, supermarkets and convenience stores sell these products in their millions every day and they are a core part of life as we know it.

We can take these everyday products for granted—until something like a pandemic comes along and makes us realise how valuable toilet paper and hand sanitisers are to us. I see a correlation between our approach to these simple items and the simple workplace scenarios we often overlook that could teach us plenty, if only we paid closer attention. That's what I strive to do in this book.

I have had a thirty-year career in marketing and selling everyday items (from Fairy Liquid to Frosties) working with great companies and well-known brands. This book sets out to share parts of my experiences and learning that I hope will be of interest and value to others, revealing simple ways to develop leadership and performance. The building of trust and respect helps everyone to perform better and feel happier in their work. Some basic interventions can deliver marginal and even add up to significant gains.

Commentary and guidance on leadership, management and analysis of the skills and competencies required to succeed in business have been published and will continue to be published over again. John Adair and Simon Sinek instantly come to my mind and if you want to understand the thoughts and philosophies of successful and revered business minds, seek out any number of books about Jack Welch, Steve Jobs or Bill Gates. Maybe even Donald Trump? Or maybe not! On the UK side of the Atlantic, take your pick from James Dyson, Alan Sugar or Allan Leighton, for example. There are thousands of biographies and autobiographies of the many visionaries, leaders of corporations and the consultants, commentators and academics who have studied them.

I have taken a different and slightly more irreverent approach. Not to denigrate industries and organisations worth trillions of pounds, or individuals who have facilitated supply of life's essentials, but to try and share learnings and insights in an easy to digest format, ideal for a flight or on a long train journey. Similar if you like to Jim Rohn and Chris Wideners' classic short story *Twelve Pillars, Baked Alaska* is an easy read.

So, carry on reading for 'warts and all' observations from someone who never quite reached the very highest levels, though worked closely with many who have. I have enjoyed my career and taken personal satisfaction from the widespread respect and popularity earned, so I'll be honest and often quite flippant, as I meander through my career and experiences.

Peter Kay has developed a phenomenally successful comedy career and a place in the nation's heart, by often just highlighting mundane events in a comedic light. His reference to "switching the big light on" at home and sales assistants in bakeries and pie shops saying "tenner going in (the till), Maureen," are comic highlights he has drawn from everyday life. There is much more to Peter's talent of course, but these are some of the building blocks of his humour. His Car Share series was a hilarious portrayal of a Supermarket Manager providing a Checkout Operator with a daily lift to work, musing on everyday occurrences. Quite apt as you read through this book. I want to share insights and occurrences from everyday business experiences to reveal simple ways of developing leadership and performance.

For obvious reasons I won't be sharing many names as the purpose is neither to laud organisational 'heroes' or embarrass those caught out when they were 'learning by doing', but I can assure readers that the situations and scenarios described were all observed by myself or passed on from reliable and trusted sources. There are a few 'myths' and 'legends' (concerning glove puppets for example), that would be difficult for me to prove, though the stories at the time were quite well articulated across the grocery trade. I may end up losing some acquaintances along the way if they recognise where I've referenced their actions in a poor light and I'm not shy of acknowledging my own mistakes either however, there are some strong lessons from telling this story so it's worth the risk. As the saying goes, "you can't make an omelette without cracking a few eggs".

The fundamental lesson is how to get the best out of the people you work for, work with and those you manage yourself. Countless theoretical tomes have been produced on people management, coaching and development. Hours and hours of research, profiles and models have been developed to help you understand yourself, your team, and the colleagues around you. There are many organisations who will determine where you are on the Insights Wheel, or how you are profiled through Myers Briggs. Different companies and managers place varying levels of importance on this type of analysis and some development tools are more useful than others, but ultimately, I would suggest that developing people isn't hard. Really, with a modicum of common sense and courtesy, it just isn't that difficult.

In business we invariably encounter situations which are not binary. There are circumstances where simple yes/no decisions (with nothing in between) are required but even matters of law or regulation can still be open to interpretation. Decisions are often based on judgement or intuition and things are rarely 'black or white'. I have always referred to this as 'playing in the grey zone'. No, I am not referring to 'sitting on the fence', 'hedging your bets' or procrastination, more a situation where there just aren't clear right or wrong outcomes. I have seen some people struggle with this concept whilst others leverage it to the advantage of their business and themselves. One of the 'Beliefs of Excellence' I was introduced to by Cecara Consulting, was that "Everyone makes the best possible choice available to them at the time".

Another of the 'Beliefs of Excellence' is that "The person with the most flexibility in thinking and behaviour, stands the best chance of success". On that basis, a lot of what I have written are *my* views and *my* interpretation of situations. Readers can judge my take on events for themselves, as though I have quoted Matthew 5:13 my views aren't 'gospel'.

I aim to provoke thought, inspire action, and hopefully provide a little levity and amusement along the way. Eager readers can learn so much more from follow up study of the theories and disciplines referenced and alluded to. With the glories of Google, greater understanding of any subject is rarely more than a few clicks away. The *Harvard Business Review* is also a fine source of revelatory thinking that has influenced my perspective in several fields.

You will notice quite a few sporting references and analogies as you read through. I apologise to those who have no interest in football (soccer) or rugby and hope they stick with the book anyway. Watching live sport has been a key part of my life and whilst I know that many find it boring, there are often similarities between sport and business, particularly in the areas of teamwork, motivation and performance.

I applied for a position as an independent non-executive director for the Professional Footballers Association in 2020. Unfortunately, I wasn't successful, but aside from the remuneration, my key motivation was a firm belief in the positive power that football can exert in society and a desire to help channel this. Most newspaper and media coverage of professional footballers tend to be about their excesses and bling lifestyles. However, look at what Marcus Rashford achieved in changing UK government policy for the benefit of disadvantaged kids. Consider the joy and love that Jermaine Defoe brought into the tragically short life of little Bradley Lowery. Also, Neville Southall has become a social justice campaigner using Twitter to highlight vulnerability and champion issues affecting many who are overlooked in society. Top sports stars often have the potential for greater positive influence than politics, religion, or the corporate social responsibility policies of large companies.

To summarise sections, I have captured *my* key thoughts and insights as simple (car) bumper stickers to ponder on. Easily digested and remembered.

Baked Alaska can't promise to divulge secrets on how to 'double your business overnight', 'guarantee step changes in performance' or 'supercharge your career progression', but it will provide honest, down- to-earth advice on how to treat people appropriately, gain their trust and respect and learn from my mistakes (and successes of course!).

Gary Vaynerchuk, chairman of Vayner X, captured similar sentiments when saying, "I'm not here to give advice, I'm here sharing experiences and observations from my life/career with the most context and clarity and consistency that I can. I'm hopeful that people take the map and build on it and use it. I'm here trying to 'win', but the trophies I'm chasing and how I go about getting them are different—I think it can help a lot of people be happier if they chase what matters to them."

I completed this work in 2020, a quite unprecedented year since the Coronavirus disrupted life as we knew it. To highlight one key positive would be the resilience shown by people across the globe. That isn't to ignore the sadness and despair, but rather to celebrate the individual, community and business resilience that came to the fore. I read a forbes.com article explaining "why the word for 2021 is resilience" and I completely agree.

LEADING PEOPLE: THE GOOD, THE BAD AND THE UGLY

"I remember the time you had recently joined, and we were on a training course. You came to partner me in an exercise, and I felt privileged to have a Senior Manager as I was the least experienced member of staff. This gave me confidence to carry on and not to give up on anything."

Mukesh, Local Business Development Manager, Barr Soft Drinks.

"You have always been so friendly, approachable and 'one of us'". The way you engage an audience is inspiring. Thanks for giving me my first break into sales at the ripe old age of forty something, a time when I really needed the confidence and financial boost."

Debra, Business Development Executive, Barr Soft Drinks.

"I just want to say thank-you! I have worked with numerous senior leaders in business and within the RAF reserve forces and I can without doubt state you have been a true inspiration. I admire your strength in character when tough decisions need to be made, yet a genuine interest in subordinates. These are qualities which are often rare within one individual, and this has made working for you a true pleasure."

Aman, Business Development Manager, Barr Soft Drinks.

"Thank-you for all that you have done to build Barr into what it is today – there was a small core of folk that came in when we were tiny and created something that others wanted to be a part of – you were key to this. You've been a consistently high-profile leader in the company with a huge following of admirers. You always look out for your people, always speak up for what is right and fair and always had time to share some advice and support. I hope that you are proud of all that you have achieved."

Stuart, Finance Director, Barr Soft Drinks.

CHAPTER 1 – BAD MANNERS

Emotional Intelligence

A standard definition of Emotional Intelligence refers to the ability to identify and manage one's own emotions, as well as the emotions of others. It is generally viewed as comprising three skills:

1. emotional awareness or the ability to identify one's own emotions
2. the ability to harness those emotions and apply them to tasks like thinking and problem solving
3. the ability to manage emotions, which includes regulating one's own emotions and helping others to do the same

Awareness of peoples' intelligence quotient (IQ) is a generally familiar concept, whereas an understanding of emotional quotient (EQ) is less well known. The importance of EQ in business has been studied and analysed comprehensively by a multitude of others, so I am going to share thoughts and observations on a basic level

I can always remember my grandmother saying that there was "no shame in being poor, but soap, water don't cost much and good manners don't cost anything". Developing that simple concept, there can be a lot to admire in someone who is fiercely committed, incredibly driven and highly successful, but it only takes a few seconds to thank others and some seldom do.

Early in my career, perhaps naively, I was quite shocked at conferences and meetings where you could be engaged in conversation with someone who would 'cut you dead' and abruptly terminate the discussion because they'd spotted an opportunity to talk to someone far more senior and influential. I have experienced people turn their back and move off mid-sentence on many occasions. It took me a while to understand what was happening and who the worst culprits were. Not only is this incredibly rude, but of course very short-term thinking. There is a good chance that your paths will continue to cross, and people may need your help, support, or input in the future. You may one day become more senior to them or even become their direct manager. There is a saying that you 'reap what you sow' and some people's short-sightedness means they often plant bad seeds or sometimes sow none at all.

Courtesy

It also never ceases to amaze me how in business, some people leave their manners at home when they head into work. People from all manner of backgrounds. For some it can appear like they are two people. Someone who is really affable outside of work, can seem to operate like a 'bastard' at their desk. Good morning, please and thank-you are often in short supply.

Contrast that type of behaviour to David Stirling, founder of the Special Air Service (SAS), renowned as the toughest of all the world's military special forces. In *SAS: Rogue Heroes the Authorised Wartime History*, author Ben MacIntyre described Stirling as "exquisitely polite to all" and "did not bark orders, he asked people to do things".

I am sure the friends and relatives of some colleagues I've encountered would be horrified if shown how they have treated others in the workplace. From lack of courtesy and rudeness through to premeditated 'political' and exploitative behaviour.

It may well be that some of these behaviours can be to cover personal inadequacy or some deep-rooted insecurity. Of course, there can also be a backdrop of genuine psychological conditions, such as anxiety or autism where someone may not be able to appreciate the impact of how they interact with others. However, many unfortunately choose to behave in these ways and still make it to the higher reaches of organisations. On occasion they will then go on to stress the importance of Emotional Intelligence in leadership after high level executive coaching, a Ted Talk or reading an article, despite having rarely exhibited any EQ themselves.

I've always been understanding and perhaps the lack of a more cynical edge has held me back, though there are many highly qualified proponents of 'Servant' or 'Alpha Leadership' models (Ken Blanchard captures this superbly) which are adamant that this is not the way to succeed in the modern world. Courtesy and consideration of others are not expensive in terms of time or money.

I recently spotted a great post on Linkedin by The Female Lead – "Character is how you treat those who can do nothing for you". Spot on!

Internal Affairs

Consider this scenario. Someone has just been appointed to a senior leadership role heading a large team. Many people are wary of them due to a perceived aggressive style in the past. Business is not great currently and morale is dipping. When arriving each morning how would you expect them to behave?

a) Stride into the building as normal avoiding eye contact, enter their personal office and close the door without acknowledging anyone else unless physically forced to.
b) Mutter a few hellos or good mornings with their head down, as they walk along into their office, then close the door and have their back to everyone.
c) Stroll in a little more casually, greet the people who are already at their desks with a bright "good morning" and engage a few in brief but pertinent conversation.

I have seen someone stick rigidly to option a) until external performance coaches suggested that b) or ideally c) would lift morale and help the individual connect with their team. Extremely basic advice that did not come cheap!

I have also witnessed individuals in quite senior positions be rude, aggressive and overly challenging to just about everyone around them and particularly derogatory to the most junior or lower grade members of staff. You can argue that in a meeting with peers, all should be able to stick up for themselves, but it rarely helps effective teamwork if one person is always going to be objectionable and difficult.

Here is another scenario. A Managing Director (MD) has an extremely sensitive announcement to release that will be distressing for many employees. As the MD, after releasing the announcement, would you?

a) Stay in your own office at headquarters and block out your diary?
b) Be a visible and reassuring presence but encourage business as usual.
c) 'Drag race' your new Ferrari down the car park as you leave early, causing people to rise from their desks to see what the noise is.

If you would take approach a) isn't that a bit lacking in courage and good manners? If the answer was c) is that because you'd be completely oblivious to the impact on others, unaware of how insensitive your actions might be, or you just don't care? You need a thick skin at times in management, perhaps even thicker the higher you get, but surely behaviour like c) is unnecessary and potentially very damaging. Unfortunately, ill-considered behaviour like this does happen.

And finally, I was once in a planning meeting where someone shared an idea which was immediately described by a senior person as "the most stupid idea I've ever heard". It became a standing joke for the individual who fortunately took it in good heart and attributed it to the eccentricity of the person saying it. Ironically, his idea was later used by the business on multiple occasions.

I am acutely aware of many of my mistakes and not afraid to highlight them. I once briefed someone on a proposed structural change just before the team meeting that they were about to lead. By relieving them of some pressure and promoting someone they had coached and developed I anticipated the proposal to be received positively. It wasn't! They interpreted it as a dilution of their role and responsibilities, which had made it very challenging for them to keep up a positive appearance through the meeting.

On another occasion, I was considering internal and external candidates for a role. Once I had made my decision, I was so focused on getting on with things that I neglected to inform the internal candidate directly that they had been unsuccessful. They found out from my public announcement about the new person coming in. This rude oversight was quite rightly highlighted to me by a colleague. Obviously, I apologised to the person concerned immediately, but this was incredibly poor form on my part. Fortunately, the person was understanding and knew it was out of character.

Anyone can make mistakes or errors of judgement. The most important aspect is to recognise, apologise, learn from them and not repeat. In the first scenario mentioned earlier, a manager returning to the unengaging behaviour once morale had improved would demonstrate a lack of sincerity. In the second scenario, arranging a Bentley test drive at the office, on the day of another serious announcement would be quite crass from my perspective!

The Sales Interface

Looking at supplier and customer relationships things have changed quite dramatically. When I started it was typically the main blue chip manufacturing companies that toured university milk rounds (careers fairs effectively) and competed to hire the 'cream of the graduate crop' and those who had studied but weren't necessarily committed, to a vocational or professional career path.

The retail and wholesale sectors had a lot of people who had worked up through their organisations, developing their skills on the job and working in stores as opposed to on campus. This at times created tension as 'canny' buyers would seek to put down 'cocky' graduates from suppliers. I even heard stories of physical altercations though it never happened to me. I was shouted at, insulted and on one occasion even threatened in a message left on my home answerphone by a store manager who had not received his stock. Some managers appeared to view their stores as their own petty fiefdom and a lot of inexperienced salespeople did not have the interpersonal skills to deal with this kind of behaviour.

In one of my first ever sales meetings I turned up with my Procter & Gamble trainer to meet the Senior Buyer at a cash & carry. None of us had met before and when my trainer explained that I would be the account manager going forward, the buyer was quite angry, complaining how he had constantly changing Procter & Gamble contacts who were too wet behind the ears", didn't understand his business and once they had learned were swiftly moved on and replaced by another and the cycle started again. I knew I needed to learn quickly and get things right. A year later when I was promoted to a new role, he apologised for the initial hard time, thanked me for all I had done and wished me well. I have always really cherished this acknowledgement. He had the guts and decency to apologise. At times humility is an only too rare commodity.

John Baines is now a very well respected, elder statesman in UK Wholesale. I like him a lot and we still reminisce about his warm and friendly welcome!

Another of my first responsibilities on joining Procter & Gamble was to manage the Batley cash & carry near Liverpool. The buyer there was a burly and quite belligerent chap renowned amongst sales reps for his dislike of graduates. I did my best to get on with him and ensure I provided the best possible service, but I was a tad nervous when my district manager was coming to work with me for the day and Batley's was a scheduled visit. A brief meeting with the buyer was littered with the f-word and various other expletives, though I did complete my meeting objectives. We then had the obligatory debrief in the car and fearing the worst I apologised for how the buyer had behaved. I was quite taken aback when he laughed and said that I'd "performed well", had "won the buyer" over and developed a good relationship – "believe me, he wouldn't have behaved like that if he didn't like you".

The district manager was true to his word as he advised me of my first step up the P&G ladder whilst we were sat in a McDonalds in Liverpool a few months later. Fantastic news for me, albeit not in a particularly glamourous setting. To be fair though, several years later when I was advised of promotion to Sales Controller level, my then boss ordered a bottle of champagne as we sat outside Ruthin Castle on a balmy summer's evening – that was more like it!

Over time the playing field of course levelled. Grocery Multiples made key appointments from within their supplier base (for example Allan Leighton at Asda was ex Mars) and competed for the top graduates to run their stores and manage head office functions, particularly buying and marketing. Over thirty years I have enjoyed some wonderful, productive relationships with contacts in my customers, working with incredibly talented people, many of whom continue to climb the career ladder. Fundamentally decent people who it has been a pleasure to do business with.

I've also encountered rude and overly aggressive types with little respect for the people with whom they interact. Constantly applying excessive pressure and effectively bullying suppliers does not make anyone a better person, nor elevate them to any kind of special status. It is unnecessary and archaic behaviour.

POINTS TO PONDER

- In simple terms, people do not respond well to rudeness and being treated 'like crap'.
- There is no need to treat colleagues or customers like something you want to 'scrape off your shoe'.
- Disagreement will always occur – you must find a way to deal with it productively.
- People 'click' with some more than others and great results can follow.
- However, even when you are not someone's 'greatest fan', discourtesy achieves little.
- You reap what you sow.
- A touch of humility has a powerful effect.
- Character is how you treat those who can do nothing for you.

CHAPTER 2 - E IS FOR LEADERSHIP

The great philosophical question I first encountered at University is "are leaders born or made?" This has been examined deeply, like David Rooke and William Torbert in the HBR who suggest that leaders are made, not born. From my perspective like most things in life the truth probably lies somewhere between them. Some show innate leadership qualities at an early age whilst others talk of voyages of development where their leadership evolvesThe answer is not black or white, it is in the grey zone.

Most businesses and particularly FMCG place great emphasis on leadership in the way they recruit and develop the people they believe will one day lead their organisations to on-going success and profit growth. The concept of leadership is introduced to children in the playground through games like "Follow the Leader" and the introduction of 'Form Captains' and Head Girl/Boy as their education develops. You could spend the rest of your life trawling through on-line material about leadership. I found a piece on taskque,com highlighting no less than fifteen traits that make great leaders (and you could still add to this list):

1. Honesty and integrity
2. Confidence
3. Inspire Others
4. Commitment and Passion
5. Good Communicator
6. Decision Making Capabilities
7. Accountability
8. Delegation and Empowerment
9. Creativity and Innovation
10. Empathy
11. Resilience
12. Emotional Intelligence

13. Humility
14. Transparency
15. Vision and Purpose

Glenn Leibowitz shared his Thirteen Traits of Exceptional Leaders and I love the way he employed plain, straightforward language. It makes them that little bit more 'down to earth' and accessible.

1. They trust you to do the job you've been hired to do.
2. They seek your advice and input.
3. They find opportunities to let you shine.
4. They recognise your contributions.
5. They have your back during tough times.
6. They are master storytellers.
7. They challenge you to do bigger and better things.
8. They express appreciation.
9. They are responsive.
10. They know when to apologise.
11. They give credit where credit is due.
12. They treat others with dignity and respect.
13. They care.

You could bankrupt yourself by buying all the books on this subject. I've read a few, such as *Effective Leadership* by John Adair, and Allan Leighton compiled *On Leadership* by talking to dozens of successful business leaders. My preference is to highlight ideas and let readers work out for themselves how to develop their own leadership style

When interviewing prospective sales managers, I often used to ask candidates to define the words leadership and strategy. Whilst stressing that there were no definitive answers, it was always interesting to observe a diverse range of understanding for words featuring so prominently in business.

The 3E Model

Procter & Gamble introduced me to the 3E model of Leadership representing:

- Envisioning
- Enabling
- Energising.

Envisioning:

Taking an idea and making it into a plan. Clarifying the concept, making it real and mapping out the steps to achieve it. Ensuring consistency of understanding, clarity of expectations and appreciation of priorities.

Enabling:

Providing tools and support materials. Ensuring the appropriate knowledge and technology is available as required. Coaching and developing the skills needed and delivering an appropriate environment to facilitate success.

Energising:

Ensuring everyone is 'up for it' by creating the right culture, ensuring role models and managers behaviour are consistent and infusing others with drive, determination, and enthusiasm.

This is the model I have invariably referenced through my career though there are many other frameworks, mostly incorporating the letter E! Procter & Gamble's 3E's can be expanded by adding Enrol and Execute. London Business School have a 5E model of:

- Envision
- Express
- Excite

- Enable
- Execute

And then you could add a whole host of other words starting with E such as Equip, Empower, Encourage, Edge, Effective, Emotive, Efficient, Explain, Effervesce…okay it is easy to get carried away but as a mental exercise readers can see how many other words beginning with E you can use in a Leadership model.

The Cost of Poor Leadership

Gina Gardiner, leading author and key proponent of enlightened leadership, and CEO of Genuinely You Ltd, highlights the impact of poor leadership from a personal, business and societal perspective. It is quite staggering—the cost of lost productivity and efficiency due to absenteeism alone is estimated at over seventy billion pounds in the UK.

It isn't that much of a surprise anymore when people get to senior positions and demonstrate poor leadership skills, poor judgement and a complete lack of appreciation for how they treat others.

The Dominic Cummings Barnard Castle 'eye test' affair during the first UK lockdown immediately springs to mind when he broke the rules on travel. I also shared a hard-hitting article on LinkedIn that I read about in *Sports Illustrated* in the wake of Greg Clarke's resignation as Football Association Chairman in November 2020. It was scathing, but I agreed with the sentiment:

"At a time when football desperately needed leadership, Clarke has been a disgrace. He lacked the subtlety to play political games, allowed himself to drift on the tides of tabloid opinion and was devoid of any moral authority. That, in little more than an hour he was able to bumble through a checklist of almost every outmoded stereotype before a parliamentary committee was only the final straw."

The concept of dark triad leadership was introduced on a coaching session I attended run by Professor Vicky Vass from the InTouch network. It is scary stuff. I highlight many examples of damaging 'leadership' behaviours throughout the book and know from experience that those who practice them often still flourish and progress in organisations.

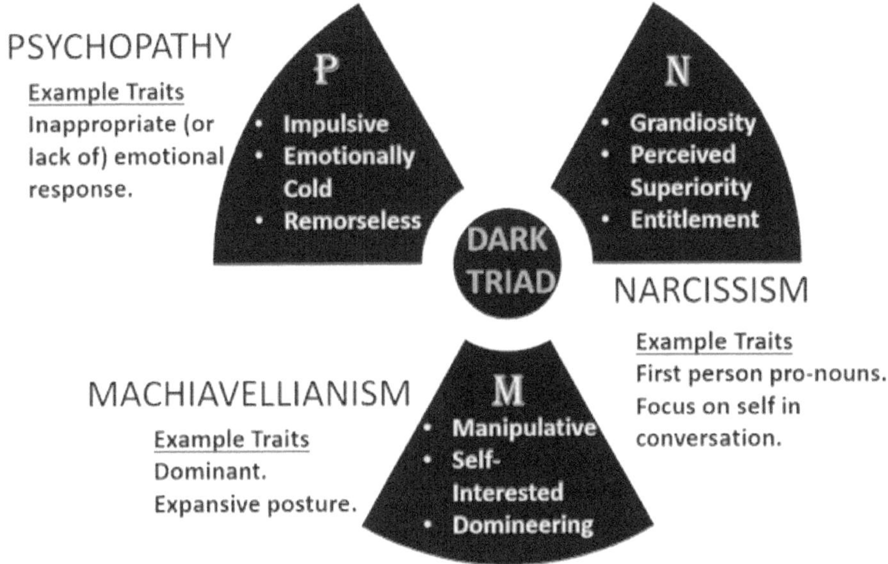

I am not suggesting that anyone I've worked with was the British equivalent of Patrick Bateman (from the film *American Psycho*), but I have witnessed some of his traits!

POINTS TO PONDER

- Leaders are born *and* made!
- Opportunities for leadership often come early.
- Speaking in plain English enables everyone.
- You cannot climb the leadership ladder without the letter E!
- Leaders require the capacity to inspire, a strong sense of purpose and social responsibility, and to lead through care and compassion, not fear and blame.

CHAPTER 3 – POWER TO THE PEOPLE

The best possible start.

Way back in 1919 William Cooper Procter continued a series of efforts to create the strongest of bonds between the Procter & Gamble Company and its employees by revising the articles of incorporation to reference that "the interests of the company and its employees are inseparable". That commitment to people certainly continued through to my joining, meaning it was a fantastic environment to start one's career. Development of people was always at the forefront and the initial training was first class. I still use skills and concepts Procter & Gamble introduced me to going way back to the pre-reading materials sent before I'd even started!

There is long list of Procter & Gamble alumni who have gone on to significant leadership roles across the globe. For example, Paul Polman who was UK MD for a spell in the nineties eventually became CEO of arch-rivals Unilever. This is of course testament to the skills and abilities of individuals, not just the training and support they receive. Jim Stengel captured this at an alumni gathering in the US when he said that "joining P&G is like joining an elite group of leaders. Its a very intense experience that stays with you long after you leave the company. Like athletic teams, P&G binds people together for their entire life"

Training

I have sat through hours and hours of training programmes during my career and a few things stand out. Firstly, the number of times I have seen the same materials (usually originating at Procter & Gamble, Mars or Unilever) adapted, developed and re-presented by others.

Secondly, I have occasionally participated with genuine awe and admiration of presenters and coaches who have shared thought provoking concepts and ideas. At Kellogg's, the Sales Director brought in a group called Cecara whose ideas were really forward thinking and their 'Beliefs of Excellence' have continually influenced my view of the world. I've also at times looked on incredulously thinking "how on earth can this person be making a living from this?" As with many situations there is the good, the bad, the average and sometimes the incredulous.

There is a saying that "those who can, do and those who can't, teach" but to be fair, I've witnessed people that I didn't particularly rate in a sales environment go on to be very effective and successful trainers. I invariably make a very quick assessment of a trainer's credibility, and I know this is probably unfair.

The General Manager of Procter & Gamble UK when I started, eventually became one of the European Vice Presidents before writing a book and facilitating a training package called 'Thinking Outside the Box'. Whilst he clearly achieved great success in his Procter & Gamble career and afterwards, I was not too impressed when I attended one of his training sessions at Kellogg's. I introduced myself and asked why he hadn't used the ideas he was presenting back at Procter & Gamble, citing some examples where we could have responded to competitive threats more effectively. I don't think he was too comfortable with my questioning and didn't really provide much of an answer.

There have been occasions where I have needed much more patience to fully appreciate the benefits someone can provide and there have also been occasions where I'm convinced that someone is 'stealing a living'.

The great thing about Procter & Gamble training was that it was invariably delivered in house, by colleagues and managers who you saw on a regular basis. That meant there was continuity of materials and most examples and role plays were appropriate to your day to day job. Often when external training companies are introduced, they 'shoehorn' the client into their existing programmes. Some do this very well as they invest time in understanding your people and business model, whilst others just put your corporate logo on the page and use the same materials for everyone.

Training programmes can also often reflect the character and views of the person who commissions the training, and they can sometimes hold quite subjective views on the people to be trained and what they require. This can at times lead to the wrong type of training organisation being used. Experienced managers often refer to their own network for training providers and I have personally seen this be very successful, but occasionally not really work with programmes cut short. I have also seen people with little experience and understanding of training and a questionable attitude to others, become manipulated by training providers. They are persuaded to invest a lot of their budget on plans that require too much, too soon from the trainees, who then become disengaged. A vicious circle can develop as people labelled as 'weak performers' are also seen as having the wrong attitude and a resistance to learning, as the original decision maker cannot accept their own misjudgement.

At Procter & Gamble training and personal development was a priority from day one. In contrast when I joined Kellogg's, the Sales team had been starved of appropriate training for several years and the new Sales Director realised that an effective training programme was essential for them to compete more effectively. He secured the investment and introduced various programmes aimed at improving functional competency and leadership amongst the more senior group. I particularly enjoyed and benefitted from the latter with insight into concepts like Alpha Leadership (in this case the art of leading consciously, captured by Robert Dilts - not to be confused with alpha male leadership styles – which may be appropriate in some environments, but in business I deplore) and the Beliefs of Excellence. The follow up one to one coaching was very enlightening and powerful.

AG Barr was different. The new Commercial Director had started to introduce some competency-based sales training which I supported when I arrived twelve months later. The prevailing culture though was that training was viewed almost as a punishment. You were sent on a training course if you were not very good at something. It took a long time to try and reverse this view and get people to understand the principles of positive, pro-active personal development as opposed to corrective, punitive activities. Occasionally, the latter perspective prevailed, ironically with some who had progressed rapidly but developed a slight sense of superiority.

One thing I have always realised about training is that there is usually way too much to remember on a course. The power is usually through the key points that 'stic" with individuals and the thoughts they provoke. A training provider used by AG Barr, Making Business Matter, differentiated their offer through a concept of reinforcing learning through 'Sticky Pieces' follow up. An innovative approach so long as the training beforehand is sufficiently spread out and doesn't take over the day job. People usually learn best at their own pace and through subsequent experience. Training rarely delivers a full improvement, 'lock, stock and barrel.'

Lattes and Learning.

Certain types of training are much better done together, face to face. However, so much training is also now on-line so why should people need to do it at their desk or in a training room? Many organisations now let their teams learn at home using eLearning and the internet. As an alternative, I introduced learning-oriented coffee mornings (hotel lobbies can be great for this).

Following the disruptions caused by the Covid19 Lockdown applications such as Zoom and Microsoft Teams have been appreciated by a much broader audience and have undoubtedly led to a change in attitudes and behaviour towards people working from home.

POINTS TO PONDER

- Some of the most effective training is delivered 'in house' as the trainers know the business and your role within it.
- Objectivity and experience are important when commissioning training.
- Training should be positive and pro-active, not corrective, or punitive.
- Focus on a few key learnings to take from training programmes, you will never remember it all.
- The best external training takes participants to a new dimension.

Coaching

Some training is quite specific to teach a process or develop a skill, but most of the learning occurs outside the 'classroom' and is most effective with a strong coach.

The International Coaching Federation (ICF) defines coaching as partnering with clients in a thought-provoking and creative process that inspires them to maximize their personal and professional potential. My purpose is not to provide extensive guidance on coaching – there are plenty of focused specialists who can do this to great effective. A few simple observations are captured below and within scenarios as we progress.

Coaching is often about providing the right support, in the right environment at the right time. To some it is almost as natural as breathing, but to others it requires more conscious effort. Procter & Gamble were very focused on managers being coaches and typically tended to excel in the field. One of the principles was that "managers should be assessed on the quality of the people they train" or words to that effect. Remarkably similar in sentiment to Simon Sinek: "the greatest contribution of a leader is to make other leaders". However, other organisations I've worked with have lacked the personnel and experience to coach successfully.

At various times I have observed managers confuse micromanagement with coaching and have become somewhat dismayed at how people have been treated and their confidence eroded. Coaching is providing freedom but keeping a supportive arm close by. It is like removing stabilisers from a child's bike and keeping hold of them as they start to pedal until they can do it themselves. It is about sharing a framework or structure and then encouraging people to use it, develop it and make it their own through timely and constructive feedback.

Coaching is not about poring over every piece of work produced, correcting, or changing trivial details and manipulating it into your own style. I despair at the times I've seen unfocused senior managers in important meetings, constantly referring to their laptops to proofread their teams' work as they lacked trust and faith in their team. Or worse, because they were so arrogant that they didn't view other's efforts as ever good enough.

Mentoring

For me, mentoring should be a very personal and natural process. I am never comfortable with the idea of mentors being appointed or allocated. For me that is too contrived and more like indirect management. A mentoring relationship usually builds on an existing personal relationship. If it needs suggesting to someone that they should mentor a junior member of the team, then I believe the point is being missed. Relationships in business can grow between people of different levels, or different functions when a connection forms naturally. Mentoring can then naturally occur without the word ever being used. If someone goes around telling others that they are a mentor to someone, I usually interpret it as looking for credit and recognition for themselves. I've supported literally hundreds of people during my career and in the vast majority of cases make sure that I'm there in a mentoring capacity if and when needed, on both a proactive and reactive basis without the M word being mentioned. Similarly, there are always people I am comfortable turning to myself for help and advice, both within my own organisation and externally.

Exploitation

On a couple of occasions, I have witnessed a situation which I've felt really uncomfortable where a senior manager in an organisation develops a friendship with a more junior and often newer employee. They do not always work on the same team, or even in the same department but the more experienced party sees skills and attributes that can enhance their own work and improve their standing in the organisation. In most cases this just develops into a genuinely supportive, mentoring relationship that benefits both.

Unfortunately, this can develop in a more sinister way where the enthusiastic, eager individual is desperately keen to impress and becomes a victim as the more senior figure finds them easy to exploit. The honest, ambitious individual is flattered by the attention and does more and more to secure recognition but eventually gets so taken advantage of that it borders on bullying. I have known people working until midnight and then being called to a manager's house over the weekend to improve and polish their presentation for a customer or a conference. The manager gets the plaudits and the individual actually gains little. The same thing can happen over and over again and whilst it might be tempting to suggest the victim should 'grow a pair' or 'man up' and refuse, saying no in business is something that many people find really hard. In my view, the more senior figure is clearly the villain and with greater emotional intelligence they would understand this is not an appropriate way to treat colleagues.

Of 'Hodds' and Men

Readers would be surprised to learn that former England football manager Glenn Hoddle had a career in FMCG! Of course, *the* Glenn Hoddle has been a football man since he signed for Tottenham Hotspur aged eight however, in terms of analogy I have witnessed his alter ego on several occasions during my career.

Without doubt Glenn Hoddle was one of the finest, most skilful, and technically gifted English players of all time, but as a coach was not able to use those skills as effectively.

The following are some quotes and commentary by players he coached/managed.

Over the years, several players have referred to his reported habit of needing to be the best on the training ground, which did little for morale. "If he were chocolate," said one England player, reportedly, "he would eat himself." The overarching impression is that here is a man who has never achieved the empathy that comes naturally to all great managers. An effective coach maybe but a manager with a tendency to belittle players for their technical limitations through his eagerness to display his own skills

Gary Neville wrote that "Hoddle took over from Venables and it's been said before: if only he had possessed the man-management skills to go with his undoubted football intelligence." It has also been said that Hoddle tends to blind his players with science, over-analysing to a point where those listening tune out. Tony Cascarino described the effect of Hoddle's man management as "grown men feel as if they are being treated as children". He would call team meetings, ask for players' input and then tell them that they were wrong.

I have had the pleasure and privilege of working with some incredibly talented and clever individuals. I really have respect for them, but no-one is ever perfect! Some have displayed 'Glenn Hoddle Syndrome' and I am sure I will have done myself on many occasions. In fact, I have done so deliberately in the Introduction, by my description of people management.

Some people are comfortable making connections with others and leading them. Many clearly are not and the idea of managing people is incredibly daunting for them. Likewise, to someone like me, building a complex interlinked spreadsheet with macros, pivot tables and complex formulas causes feelings of trepidation, to put it mildly! What is not hard for some, maybe terrifying for others.

There is a common phrase that you "shouldn't take people for granted". To expand on that, nor should you take people's innate skills and abilities for granted as this can leave them frustrated, with diminished confidence and insecure.

The point Glenn Hoddle types need to consider, but are often blind to, is the impact they have on others. Colleagues and sub-ordinates (great modern word - not!) can be left feeling demotivated and that they aren't really valued. Like Glenn, there can be a tendency for managers to show 'one-upmanship' – where they seem compelled to 'out do' others in meetings by pointedly sharing new insightful data or updates that are not always necessary or add little value.

In addition, they will often let people talk or make a point, then just move straight on to something else without even acknowledging what they have just heard. This leaves people feeling confused or belittled as they have not even been listened to.

Reference to Hoddle again – "he couldn't appreciate how those he was coaching just couldn't see what he was suggesting (vision) and do it naturally (technical skills)" words in brackets added by myself. Some managers often ask or 'throw' work at people accompanied by the phrase "it'll only take you ten minutes or so". The manager may well be able to bash it out quickly, but it may take half a day or more for someone else and often comes on top of their existing workload. This just demonstrates a lack of appreciation of others' capacity and capability.

I have tended to be too trusting in people at times and have maybe shown a bit of 'Hoddlism' when assuming that people understand what I want or need them to do. If you ask someone to do something they *can't* do, that is a capability issue, and you need to provide knowledge and support the skills required. If it is something they *won't* do, you have an attitude and motivation issue to address. Sometimes we all need to take a step back and put ourselves in other people's shoes

POINTS TO PONDER

- Micro-managing is not coaching.
- The most effective mentoring develops naturally from personal relationships.
- Providing opportunities to others is crucial but, taking advantage of others enthusiasm is deplorable.
- Everyone is unique. Recognise that we all have different strengths and weaknesses.
- Leaders and coaches should set the right example and keep raising the bar however, not by continually 'outdoing' their own team.
- Determine if performance issues are 'can't do' or 'won't do' and respond accordingly.

Feedback

Feedback and constructive criticism were early introductions in my Procter & Gamble career. The concepts had been introduced a long time before and whilst less formal feedback was an on-going component of coaching, more formal broad-based feedback as it was known, was a familiar process at performance review time. Seeking feedback on how you operated from peers, managers, and others you interacted with soon became the norm. However, actually capturing the feedback in a clear yet constructive and diplomatic way challenged some more than others. At Procter & Gamble the feedback was open and transparent so you could see how others viewed you. One person was particularly direct with feedback and caused a bit of an incident by writing in a close colleague's feedback that "Mick has a tendency to just piss people off". The recipient was aggrieved and the writer somewhat indignant. The aim should be to be honest and direct, but also polite. Such nuances escaped many!

A phrase developed that 'feedback is a gift' and should be appreciated, but to me the value only came if it was considered and well communicated feedback. I agree that feedback can be a gift, but you can choose whether to unwrap it and then still decide whether you will actually play with it. I have seen examples of terribly conceived feedback where the intent was positive, but the impact quite destructive. I have also observed feedback being used to 'stick the knife in' or belittle others.

Whilst comfortable and familiar with the concept at Procter & Gamble, at Kellogg's and latterly AG Barr the introduction was quite a revelation. Various feedback methods, sometimes deployed at different hierarchical levels are used by training companies and personal coaches the world over. *360 Degree* feedback is common terminology and can be a very, very in-depth process typically facilitated on-line by third parties from outside your own organisation. More simplistic versions include *What Went Will/Even Better If* (WWW/EBI) feedback and *Stop, Start, Continue*.

At Kellogg's, the first formalised feedback was anonymous. You selected a range of immediate peers, your boss, your direct reports, and others you work with to provide the feedback. Clearly you could work out your boss's comments and occasionally identify others by their writing style. One particularly challenging and often quite obstreperous individual was too lazy to shift between upper and lower cases, so you always knew what they'd said as it was all in capitals!

AG Barr was very different. The Commercial Director and I, who was also ex Procter & Gamble, had developed an informal feedback culture across the sales team and his comment that "feedback is a gift" was well established, though sometimes in a jocular manner! However, it was only after about ten years that the organisation considered itself ready to introduce a more formal feedback process. Some interesting discussions took place to determine whether all the people were capable of receiving and acting on feedback appropriately. I often rolled my eyes at some dismissive and patronising attitudes to colleagues and the people that individuals managed.

When required to ask for feedback I always wanted to ensure I'd get a good balance from the people I naturally gravitated towards and those I didn't connect with quite as well or see 'eye to eye' with. I am not aware of anyone exclusively choosing from the latter group, but many deliberately set out to get the feedback from their 'mates' or those they saw in the same self-image. To me this just seemed like insecurity and not really embracing the principles. If two people at the same level in an organisation do essentially the same role, why would they not ask each other for feedback? Insecurity or arrogance?

When I received feedback, I usually divided the opportunities to improve (negative comments) into three broad areas. Firstly, something I considered essentially true and my own self-awareness confirmed that I needed to work on. Secondly, something I hadn't really recognised myself, but was insightful feedback and I should consider. Finally, there is the feedback that you honestly just don't agree with. I always believe that if you have strong self-awareness and personal consciousness you have the right to dismiss it.

When asked to give feedback on an individual I always made sure to give it due thought and consideration so that it would be of value and encourage the recipient, even if I didn't feel qualified to say a lot. On some occasions it is also fair to decline an invitation if you really do not feel you can add value or insight. My general approach is to use real life examples to support the feedback, but you must get the balance right. Too much praise and positive examples can risk inflating someone's ego. Too much criticism can destroy a person's confidence. I once needed to give stern guidance on one of my team's feedback to their direct report. For every positive point (and there weren't that many) there was a brief supporting example. For the many negative points/areas to improve there were about three in depth examples every-time. The feedback made an average to good performer with a positive attitude, look like a completely useless operator and caused them significant personal distress.

When I had to include Next Higher Manager comments on someone's review or manager feedback as part of 360, I always took time to read through beforehand and reference points people had acknowledged themselves. This shows that you have paid attention and aren't just projecting your own thoughts and insights on to them. I have witnessed managers routinely just add pretty much standard comments to everyone's reviews, or a set of comments not referencing any of the individual or managers commentary – a lazy approach that deprives the recipients of the opportunity to learn.

Some remain quite sceptical about the value of 360 Degree feedback. To me it is a very powerful tool, but relies heavily on honesty, self-awareness and good communication skills. Without those factors it can be damaging.

Finally there is the potential for people to manipulate the use of feedback to try and enhance their own position rather than help to develop others. I was particularly irked by one manager who used to encourage his team to share their 'wins' and achievements for the week on a Friday afternoon. They would conclude their week with an email summarising the progress they had made and the challenges on the horizon. This was good practice in sharing learning, celebrating success and developing an *esprit de corps*. I was on the copy list and would occasionally recognise performance and results that caught my eye.

Unfortunately, the leader of this team had an incredibly annoying habit of reading through them all on a Saturday morning, giving 'feedback' to each sender. This all sounds quite admirable however, I wasn't convinced that it was because he had too much to do and no time during the week. To me it was more a disingenuous demonstration of commitment to the cause, to show how dedicated he was. The actual feedback provided was literally "Good job, well done" to each report, mostly not even personalised to the individual and invariably not specifically responding to anything that was reported. It was just lazy and added no value at all. Whilst some of the junior members of the team may have been 'thrilled' by warm words from the manager, most just saw it for what it was - cheap.

POINTS TO PONDER

- Feedback is a gift but, you can choose whether to unwrap it!
- Providing feedback is to help someone to improve, never to 'score points'
- Feedback should be provided properly or declined politely! There should be NO in between!!
- When providing feedback to others, remember the wise words of Yoda, the diminutive Jedi Knight from Star Wars: "Do or do not. There is no try"

The MacGregor Dilemma

Whilst management and motivational theory continues to be developed and I make no claims of academic excellence in the field, I have always found there to be real merit in some of the simpler, more historical theories espoused by the likes of MacGregor and Maslow, which from my experience continue to be relevant today.

Writing in the early 1960's, Douglas MacGregor developed his contrasting Theory X and Theory Y model that explained how managers' beliefs about what motivates their people can affect their management style. Theory X is the authoritarian approach and

Theory Y is much more participative.

Those who believe that team members inherently dislike work and have little motivation, then, according to McGregor, they are likely to use an authoritarian style of management. This approach tends to be very 'hands-on' and usually involves micromanaging people's work to ensure that it gets done 'properly'. McGregor called this Theory X.

On the other hand, those who believe that people take pride in their work and see it as a challenge are more likely to adopt a participative management style. Managers who use this approach trust their people to take ownership of their work and do it effectively by themselves. This is Theory Y.

Experience suggests to me that X and Y are really endpoints on a spectrum. Again, if X is white and Y is black, there is a lot of grey in between. Different types of work (physical, manual, analytical, cerebral), different work environments (public sector, private sector, large established corporations, SMEs, Entrepreneurial businesses etc) and different motivators and reward structure can all influence behaviours towards X or Y. Similarly, different challenges or situations can require a flexibility of style and approach. For example, more Theory X behaviours may need demonstrating when a crisis mentality is required, and people need to carry out specific instructions or complete tasks efficiently and effectively. A typically more Y orientated manager may need to adopt a more 'hands-on approach' at this point, but where interpersonal relationships are strong, this temporary style would be understood and accepted.

The American military introduced the acronym 'VUCA', standing for volatile, uncertain, complex and ambiguous, to describe the context of terrorist attacks and the Gulf War in the noughties. VUCA has since been applied to the rapidly changing business world with David Snowden and Mary E. Boone suggesting in the HBR that 'wise executives tailor their approach to fit the complexity of the circumstances they face'. Their work on the Cynefin framework explores this concept in much greater detail than I could summarise here.

Another area of growing debate surrounds consistency. Jack Welch once claimed that great leaders are 'relentless and boring' by remaining on-message, sticking to their commitment and demonstrating consistency in their decision-making. Another article I read in the HBR shares the principle of 'both / and' leadership and how in the modern (VUCA) world leaders shouldn't worry so much about being consistent as at the top, executives and leaders must be able to appreciate multiple, often conflicting truths. Again, I refer to the grey zone where I fully agree with the sentiment when the tailoring or inconsistency is sincere and constructive.

What frustrated me from time to time though, was seeing fellow managers engage in 'double speak'. In a managerial forum, some would clearly position themselves as advocates of Theory Y, for example, pushing a training agenda, talking about career development for individuals and improving organisational effectiveness. They would then go back to working with their teams and revert to Theory X! I've worked with people in my career who almost seemed to have a split personality. They would 'wax lyrical' publicly about the importance of training, coaching and mentoring and then display very little understanding of what it meant day to day by micro-managing people, making 'snap' judgements on individuals potential (or lack of) and at times remaining aloof and dismissive of their direct reports and other colleagues.

Whether this type of behaviour is born of arrogance, insecurity, an absence of self-consciousness or at times a deliberate tactic to 'unsettle' or 'keep people on their toes' can be debated and of course will vary by individual. However, the impact on those they lead could be damaging. One person I worked with acquired the semi-jovial nickname of 'Der Fuhrer' by some of their team and when challenged about this insisted that they were quite happy with it!

POINTS TO PONDER

- Typically, people respond best to consistent styles and behaviours from their leaders.
- In a VUCA world, strong leadership can require flexibility and tailoring of approaches so that 'sincere inconsistency' can be constructive.
- 'Insincere inconsistency' is disrespectful and tantamount to playing games with people.
- Strong leadership can require flexibility in management style.
- Practice what you preach!

Hexagonal Pegs

In many organisations, people join a specific function, in a specific role and often become labelled with that i.e. "She's an operations person" or he is a "sales guy", "they're just a marketeer" and so on. On joining Procter & Gamble as a graduate I joined the Sales Department and that was where my career and progress was mapped out. There could be movement between functions but typically that was later in a career when someone had consistently demonstrated their ability. There were several movements from Sales across to Marketing as people wanted to broaden their skill set for a move into General Management. Whilst at Kellogg's the Sales Finance partner actually moved across permanently and became a very good National Account Manager, before quitting for a much bigger job back in finance. Some companies recruit onto a "graduate program" where they initially spend time working in a variety of functions and then in conjunction with their management and Human Resources, they focus on the area deemed the best fit. Clearly there are merits and drawbacks to each approach.

It is not just on a departmental basis that some get labelled though. Within the sales environment colleagues and peers have been identified as a "numbers guy" or a "people person" or someone who is only "good with customers" and not seen to have strong enough leadership qualities to progress. A recurring descriptor to "pigeonhole" someone is: "not strategic enough". I have had that one a few times.

Of course, we do all have different skill sets and natural abilities and moving people between roles is not necessarily the right thing to do. In a business, like Procter & Gamble who work hard to recruit "top talent" most people join with ambitions to make it to the very top. It is over time that labels are picked up and many people are happy with their label. The person who loves the "cut and thrust" of selling to customers can sometimes have little interest or motivation to do a more planning or analytical role. Similarly, some people in sales just love managing and developing teams of salespeople and do not actually want to spend too much time in front of customers. Someone from my early days in sales at Procter & Gamble, eventually progressed to a Global Marketing HR role elsewhere.

Historically people were reluctant to "nail their colours to a particular (job) mast" through fear of being seen as unambitious or not supporting the broader organisational needs. Over time, thankfully there tends to be more support and encouragement for people to be open and honest about the parts of the job they enjoy and want to do. The most mature accept that this could limited their opportunity to progress but accept the compromise.

For example, Jo Bloggs is strong in certain areas making her a "square peg", but there are plenty of "square hole" roles in the business so she can continue to grow. Jack Bloggs is very much a "round peg". There aren't many round "holes" in the business, so they'll have to spend some time in a square hole if they want to progress further.

I was always uncomfortable with people being labelled in this way by others. Particularly when managers who had never worked with the individuals could have quite an input to their career. I have heard managers with vacancies to fill say "I'm never having x in my team because they are only good at this, or not good at that". My view was always that the manager should take responsibility to develop the areas where someone was weaker, not be dismissive and write them off.

Despite my protestations, I have been frustrated on occasions by someone else's preconceived ideas and intransigent views about a person, being used to block them moving into a role. This often tends to be found in those who have limited experience of developing people over time and accelerated progression later in their own careers. I have taken belated satisfaction from this scenario on several occasions, when those I have trained and supported have proved any doubters wrong!

Using the traditional example of square/round pegs and holes you could get too carried away and assign all manner of shapes to individuals and roles within a business, but that could get a bit silly. I would however draw attention to what I call a "hexagonal peg". This is someone who has incredible ability and can be squeezed into a round hole or a square hole, but never quite fits. I have witnessed a few great talents who weren't considered as "sales" people or viewed as a "true marketeer" and moved through various commercial roles never fully delivering against their own, or the organisation's expectations. For this reason, they often don't progress as fast as peers with less ability and some managers don't have the patience or understanding to find them the right role. My view is simple – "hexagonal pegs" are few and far between. If you ever find you have one, invest the time and energy to identify a hexagonal hole and it will invariably pay great dividends!

POINTS TO PONDER

- You may have to make some compromises at points on the career journey but need to be clear on your strengths and what you enjoy.
- The best managers embrace responsibility for improving all members of their team.
- If you inherit or unearth a hexagonal peg – cherish and invest in them!

Seeing the Results

Ultimately, seeing people you have recruited, trained, and developed progress in your organisation and often go on to even bigger and better achievements is one of the best feelings in a business career. I've been in training and managerial positions pretty much since year one with Procter & Gamble and whilst there have been the odd individuals who I struggled to connect with, or very rarely, didn't like at all, seeing people grow and develop has given me immense personal satisfaction and a real sense of accomplishment that financial reward and promotions genuinely don't match up to.

AG Barr was the biggest source of satisfaction as I was there the longest and in a senior position. Given it wasn't a 'grad culture' there were many examples of people joining at sixteen or with few formal qualifications, who had great potential, but just needed backing and support to progress. Several of these 'Ugly Ducklings' grew into 'Beautiful Business Swans'! They embraced change and bought into the training and coaching we introduced. Their own talent and natural abilities, combined with a high work ethic, deservedly elevated them to the most senior positions in the Sales Function.

As ever, Procter & Gamble introduced me to a formula that captures this – the KSA model. Performance is driven by the Knowledge, Skills and Attitude of the individual. In AG Barr, the Ugly Ducklings had great knowledge of the business and great attitudes, what we were able to do was drive their skills and competencies through a focus on development. And off they went to secure some outstanding achievements!

Of course, that isn't to say that graduates are any less worthy of praise however, a university degree usually allows people to commence a career higher up the ladder. Their expectations are typically more overt than the bright people who haven't previously been encouraged or supported and hence have more covert ambitions. These individuals need a catalyst and I was privileged and delighted to provide it.

Recognition

Recognition is often discussed (certainly in HR terms) with Reward or Remuneration, though this discussion is just about the importance of recognising a job well done, or someone's real efforts and commitment. Over many years I have looked upwards in organisations and been quite disappointed when concluding that the most senior levels in a business often just take people for granted. Some would say that people are paid to do a job and may receive bonuses determined by performance of the Company and/or themselves. So why should they need or be given extra?

A fair point in many respects, but I am not concerned here about financial reward, more the human side of recognition and that simple emotion – gratitude.

Not long after joining Procter & Gamble I recall an occasion where one of the most venerable members of the Sales Department, very senior to me at the time, but nowhere near the top of the organisation was retiring. Through his long career he had supported and encouraged the development of many of those currently climbing upwards. At one of his final meetings his direct reports presented him with a shirt of Everton Football Club, with his name and retirement age printed on the back. This was the early nineties, before the internet and easy ordering of such items, so it must have taken quite a bit of effort to arrange it. I remember thinking to myself what a lovely gesture this was and wondering if anything like that would ever happen to me in the future.

At one Procter & Gamble meeting just before Christmas, when the Division Manager opened the day in the morning, after running through the agenda he called me up to the front. I wasn't sure why, but he proceeded to recognise my contribution through the year, thanked me for my efforts and handed me a bottle of champagne. I was thrilled with this recognition and returned to my seat beaming. He than called up someone else to do similar and across the day everyone was given a bottle of champagne. It was a lovely touch, but of course nobody ended up feeling particularly special!

Being American multi-nationals, both Procter & Gamble and Kellogg's had rather 'twee' (to those in the UK) formalised recognition programs. Procter & Gamble's had the grandiose title of Global Chairman's Club Award or something similar. One of my managers and long-time mentor was flown to Head Office in Cincinnati to accept one of these awards and I'm sure it meant a huge amount to him, but most people were not 'turned on' by the Global Chairman's Award. It was based on submissions from each country, without any real transparent criteria so most regarded it as a 'political' device and retained a level of cynicism. Kellogg's had a similar type scheme and though I was part of a team that won one for a World Cup In-store promotion in 2002, there was no trip to the States and the prize of a golden statuette of Kellogg's founder invariably provoked a degree of mirth and mockery.

Retailers and Wholesalers also often issue 'Awards' to Suppliers and the first one I ever received did really mean a lot at the time. Procter & Gamble's UK Sales Vice President contacted me one day to congratulate me as he had been sent an award from Asda CEO Allan Leighton to recognise a project, Toiletries Champions that my team and I had executed across Asda's store portfolio. The VP was impressed with the project results and the ABCD (Above and Beyond the Call of Duty) Award that had been sent through. This was typically an Asda internal recognition and so we were one of the first suppliers to ever receive one. Later Asda started to, in a colleague's words, "hand them out like confetti to every Tom, Dick and Harry" at Supplier Conferences. This was a little bit of a sour comment, but certainly they did become distributed by Buyers and Buying Managers, not sent from the CEO to Sales Vice Presidents.

Other customers also used Awards at Conferences and Gala Dinners, but again, many viewed them quite cynically as there was no transparency and most considered them meaningless or just a reflection of who had invested the most promotion monies or 'sucked up' to the Buying Team. The two awards we had great success with at AG Barr were very different.

The Bestway Wholesale Supplier of the Year and the Top Supplier Award from the Scottish Wholesale Association (SWA) both had open and clear scoring and adjudication and also included votes from staff working in the branches and cash and carries. They had clear, objective criteria and did not rely on arbitrary decisions behind closed doors. I take huge pride and satisfaction from leading teams who won both these awards on numerous occasions.

Awards like Bestway and SWA were presented at Black Tie Gala dinners where the emphasis was literally on 'celebrating success' a phrase that became more and more common in the later stages of my sales career, though I'd say it was more of a 'buzz' phrase, often used without true conviction.

The most exhilarating example of celebrating success I witnessed was one afternoon in the mid-nineties when I was in Asda House in Leeds. Asda was still a plc at the time, prior to being acquired by Walmart. CEO Allan Leighton had been presenting Asda's latest results to analysts in The City that morning and was heading into the office to brief everyone. Asda had great momentum at the time and was on a run of being able to report the "fastest like for like sales growth in the industry". Asda House has a large open Atrium with balconies over-looking it on all four sides and as Leighton arrived, the balconies all the way up were filled with a noisy exuberant crowd. It was a bit like being in an indoor arena for a music concert. As he stood with a microphone on the ground floor looking up and congratulating the Asda colleagues on another great set of performance figures the atmosphere was absolutely electric. You could feel the energy and excitement buzzing all around!

Contrast that with the somewhat more conservative, restrained environment at AG Barr. On one occasion when we had delivered our best performance to date and were becoming highly regarded by analysts and investors in The City, at the first Management Board Meeting of the new year, a tray of bacon rolls was brought up to the boardroom to recognise the successful prior year. To be fair, the CEO had also arranged for a fried egg roll recognising that one of the team did not eat meat. Inspiring stuff!

Opus Dei

Metaphorically, at times I used to feel that Barr was like the FMCG branch of 'Opus Dei' with a predilection for corporal mortification. We delivered some fantastic results over many years though some people seemed more excited and stimulated by a crisis when they could set up 'War Rooms' or 'Cobra Committees' to pore over problems and their dire implications. Pleasure and satisfaction seemed almost 'frowned' upon versus the deep-rooted gratification taken from trying to fix various setbacks.

On one occasion I worked with an HR colleague on a project to help managers understand simple ways they could acknowledge and recognise good work. I was surprised at how the culture had developed in some of the other functions and was a little incredulous at how some managers barely saw the need to even say 'thank-you' and extend common courtesies. One of the techniques I had regularly used of sending a £10 Gift Card and thank-you note to someone's home address was seen by some as outlandish and unnecessary. A few in a year would hardly mean a profit warning and recipients were typically very grateful.

At a corporate level Barr was a little introverted however, salespeople enjoyed a bit more noisy and extrovert recognition, so I introduced some light-hearted Sales Awards at our annual National Sales Meeting. Some awards were more serious and nominated by people's managers, but the real fun was when we got into 'Most bizarre choice of Company Car' and 'Best Dressed' awards. These awards were a tad 'tongue in cheek' and the result of opaque deliberations, but I did see people referencing titles like 'Best Business Result' and 'Best Newcomer' in their performance reviews and even on their CV. However, it was possibly the bottle of Prosecco that was most appreciated.

When Success is Not Celebrated

> 'The greatest gift of leadership is a boss
> who wants you to be successful'—Jon Taffer

One of the Procter & Gamble principles that stuck with me was that managers should be assessed on the quality of the people they recruit, train and develop. I have always taken an immense amount of pride and pleasure in seeing people who I once trained, or who worked in my team, go on to wonderful achievements. Many of those I've coached have gone on to have fantastic careers, leaving my progression in their slipstream as they have risen to the highest levels of global organisations, founded and developed their own businesses and been successful MDs and entrepreneurs. I consider it a privilege to have played some part, however small or brief, in helping them get there. I never, ever resent their success.

Unfortunately, there are some people that I call 'Uncle Joes'—referring to Franklin Roosevelt's nickname for Josef Stalin. Uncle Joes occupy positions of influence and control over others, are sometimes quite dour and invariably resentful and suspicious. They value and appreciate the results that their top people deliver, but they inwardly dislike the respect and popularity that charismatic and successful people build with those around them.

Sometimes it gets to the point where they resent a person so much that they seek to marginalise or remove them, even if that comes at the detriment of performance and organisational culture. This isn't just at lower or middle management levels; it can go right to the very top.

At the end of the Second World War, Field Marshall Zhukov was recognised, lauded and celebrated as the man whose military exploits had freed Mother Russia from the Nazis. Stalin had publicly thanked him forty-one times during the conflict. He was the people's saviour, a hero of the Soviet Union. He had a bright future.

So, what did Uncle Joe do?

Celebrate him? Reward him? Fete him?

No!

Stalin banished him into obscurity.

Zhukov got lucky. Stalin could have just as easily had him removed 'for good'. Once Stalin had died, Zhukov was able to return.

Some people in leadership positions constantly feel threatened. They don't have the ability or awareness to truly appreciate, harness and utilise those whose skill set is different from their own. Particularly when it comes to managing and motivating others. To them, power is power. The concept of 'vulnerability is power' is as alien as the landscape on Jupiter. Despite someone's strong track record and what they contribute to the bottom line, rather than developing them and driving a positive culture, they choose to just get rid of them.

Who'd want to work for Uncle Joe?

POINTS TO PONDER

- People appreciate being appreciated. They don't appreciate feeling taken for granted.
- Money is clearly important however, there are other effective forms of recognition.
- Sometimes just the words 'thank-you' are enough.
- Awards can offer huge motivation but can also have the opposite effect.
- The most credible awards have clear objective criteria.
- Watch out for Uncle Joe.

CHAPTER 4 – BAKED ALASKA

Reflecting on University and my Business Studies degree I recall being a little perplexed in the Management of Operations module when we discussed the different roles that being part of an organisation can fill for people. The one that stood out was the whole sense of belonging and personal security idea where an organisation can act as a 'comfort blanket'. Over time I came to realise what this meant and on my final day with AG Barr someone captured the concept perfectly.

Just after I joined, we moved the offices out of a relatively decrepit factory into brand new modern office space on Middlebrook Business Park just near to Bolton Wanderers' stadium. The board appointed me as the site leader, to manage the transition and act as the figurehead for all departments on the site going forward. It wasn't perfect (at one point you could never get a parking space!) but overtime we developed a great environment where people were generally very happy to come to work. Simple, little things made a difference. I always toured the office at some point each day just to say hello, check how people were and ensure that everyone, not just my direct reports, were comfortable to approach me if needed. Obvious things like a Christmas lunch, night out and office donuts from time to time were of course well received. Over time we reached Investors in People (IIP) Silver status and invariably recorded the highest site scores in the company's annual Employee Engagement Survey.

On that last day, one person who'd had more than their fair share of personal setbacks told me that getting through those challenges had a lot to do with coming into the Middlebrook office, which was described as a 'sanctuary' and thanked me sincerely for providing the leadership which had created it. I had feelings of intense pride and a true sense of fulfilment when I heard this. It was possibly my most poignant lesson in motivation since I first tried Baked Alaska.

The Dessert Menu

I had joined Procter & Gamble straight from University after a summer as a Holiday Rep for Saga (working with elderly people really did teach me a lot about patience and maturity!). After a year as an Account Executive working in field sales, I was promoted and joined the Grocery Discount Team working for a seasoned sales manager who'd single-handedly developed Kwik Save into a major customer. He was now about to hand over some responsibility to a new inexperienced account manager and I knew he was a little nervous. Kwik Save had a very aggressive reputation, and he didn't want me messing up the business.

I was desperate to impress him and paid avid attention during training for the role. We spent a lot of time together and got to know each other quite well. I remember telling him once in conversation that I'd always been fascinated by the dessert Baked Alaska as to make it, you put ice cream into a hot oven. However, I had never actually tried it.

A few months later we had an out of office 'away day' where we stayed overnight in a nice hotel in Northumbria. The hotel had printed a bespoke menu for our meeting and the dessert was Baked Alaska. I looked at my boss who returned me a warm smile. He had listened, remembered and made a relatively simple gesture, but I'd have run through a brick wall at that point if he'd asked me. Metaphorically, I slept wrapped in a warm comfort blanket that night.

The Power of the Pizza

Not long after Baked Alaska, I started to appreciate the importance of another culinary item in building a sense of belonging – I call it 'The Power of The Pizza'. Like many offices and workplaces, when we had a lot of people on-site for meetings, a buffet lunch would be provided. Some would tuck in without reserve whereas others (me included) would pick and fuss at whether the sandwiches had cucumber or mayo on them or grumble that the crisps were only ready salted. Some people would ignore the buffet completely or bring their own lunch as usual. In the end there was always waste. I am sure that most readers will have experienced something similar.

One day I asked the PA responsible for the site if we could have pizza delivered instead of a buffet. As the delivery arrived the smell of pizza drifted through the office. Virtually everyone wandered from their desk to the meeting area, filled their face with pizza and chatted together for fifteen minutes or so. There was a spark in the office that day and not even a slice of green pepper was left over. Ever since, over nearly thirty years I've often deployed the Power of the Pizza at team meetings and office briefings – it brings people together like nothing else (there's always someone who doesn't like pizza though, so order a few portions of wedges and nuggets too!)

N.B. Krispy Kreme Do-nuts also work well and were set up in the UK by another Procter & Gamble alumni!

The Wild Geese

As I developed through my Procter & Gamble career I eventually headed up my first full sales team from a site right on the edge of the Procter & Gamble world at Skelmersdale, Lancashire where they had a Health and Beauty products distribution centre, also home to the small northern National Accounts team which I was appointed to lead. The team essentially consisted of a couple of experienced, wily campaigners mixed with a sprinkling of eager and enthusiastic graduates (including Greg Jackson the founder and CEO of Octopus Energy) and a wonderful Personal Assistant (PA). The three and a half years I had there were magical – I learned so much and had great fun.

As a small team based 'up north' out of site of the head office in Weybridge, Surrey we were quite autonomous, effectively 'off the grid' and within reason could behave as we wished. We worked hard, delivered some excellent results and didn't take ourselves too seriously.

After seeing a fabulous video produced by Saatchi & Saatchi in New Zealand at a planning meeting, I persuaded them to get me a copy to share with the team as I truly believed that it reflected the way the team was operating. The video was *Lessons from Geese* and anyone can now see versions of it on Youtube. The original Saatchi version still brings a lump to my throat as the team embraced it as an authentic representation of our working philosophy and modus operandi.

An idea came from within the team that we should use the Geese analogy to create a team vision and mission statement. Everyone in the team had input and we re-worked and word-smithed it until everyone was happy before getting it professionally printed. It then took pride of place in our office and on our desks. The UK General Manager came to visit the site and was enthusiastic about the culture and 'down to earth' environment we had developed.

One of the ideas we took from Asda was the idea of a red baseball cap to wear at your desk as a 'do not disturb' sign when you were concentrating on something. One of the team took the initiative to get personalised caps for each of us. Mine was embroidered with Saint Steve—well, I am from St Helens after all!

When the next General Manager was appointed, he shared with everyone his vision for how he wanted the business to run, the type of environment he wanted to create and the support and co-operation we needed to share. His comments closely mirrored what we had created so I sent him a copy. I never received any feedback and moved on from Procter & Gamble just after.

Tea, or is it Dinner?

One instance that genuinely hurt was at one of my first sales conferences. In the afternoon break, I remarked to a colleague that I was really hungry and wondered "what we would be having for tea?" A more senior figure who I hardly knew turned around and said quite sneeringly "Tea? Tea? Good Lord you're working for Procter & Gamble now. Your evening meal is called *dinner*". Whilst maybe trivial to some the effect of this 'put down' did linger (and still does) and drove at the heart of my personal insecurity. I didn't feel a great sense of belonging to Procter & Gamble that day and on a later training course learned that this was probably an example of tertiary discrimination. Ever since, I have always endeavoured to give new starters a warm and inclusive welcome, whichever organisation I worked for.

Acronyms

I have often heard said that joining a new business can be like learning a new language as all organisations have their own phrases, terminology and particularly anacronyms. And that is before you get to know the dynamics of the marketplace and the characteristics of the brand or products. It can be difficult to fit in and remember what everything stands for, but typically you get there over time. Once you are familiar with the business language and colloquialisms you start to feel a greater sense of belonging. FMCG is full of acronyms – a unique language with individual company dialects.

Tony's Weekly Award for Teamwork

Acronyms do also occasionally provide an opportunity for mischievous or immature fun. We had a weekly 'huddle' in Kellogg's (the idea being borrowed from Asda) where everyone in the sales team who was in the office would come together to share important updates and celebrate success. Either the Sales Director or one of the Sales Leadership Team (SLT) would lead the session and after a while someone suggested that we should recognise individuals' contribution to the team more formally. Again, inspiration came from Asda who had introduced a golden cone parking system years before, where great results or strong performance would be recognised by reserved parking at the front of the building or use of the company Jaguar for the week. All agreed it was a good idea, but it needed a name or identity. Kellogg's liked to bring their brand characters to life across the business, so with Frosties in mind I suggested Tony's Weekly Award for Teamwork. After a while someone realised how this would convert to an acronym!

A colleague later brought up in an SLT meeting that they were really pleased that one of the team, who had never appeared particularly engaged with the business had really responded to the Huddle and had been spotted taking notes. Impressed and intrigued one of the Sales Controllers elected to stand near them at the next one and peered over their shoulder as they wrote. I don't remember the exact details, but the notepad apparently read something like: Frozen Cod, Minced Beef, New Potatoes, 2x Beans, Fairy Liquid, Bread Rolls, Cheese etc. They was actually writing a shopping list, far from engaged at all!

Agent of Change

One of the reasons I had been recruited by Kellogg's was to support a cultural change. As a market leading, US multinational I had expected Kellogg to be similar to Procter & Gamble in terms of culture, systems and business processes. They were both supporters of huge iconic brands with high levels of marketing investment and a commitment to Research & Development. However, I think it is quite fair to say that in many ways Kellogg's was way behind Procter & Gamble. It had been quite staid, autocratic and did not seem particularly committed to Learning and Development and career pathing. The new Sales Director had been an internal appointment and was keen to modernise the department's thinking. In contrast to Procter & Gamble, Kellogg were always prepared to also recruit externally.

For a period before my arrival, the UK Head Office in Old Trafford had apparently been 'over-run' by Management Consultants, helping to devise a strategy and implement a plan to transform the old approach to a New Kellogg that was more fit for the future. This had involved some re-structuring with job losses through early retirement and roles becoming redundant, whilst new roles were identified to be filled from within or externally (hence my arrival).

At this time, as the new millennium beckoned the grocery marketplace was undergoing quite radical change as Tesco continued to strengthen, Asda had been acquired by Walmart, Sainsbury were trying to define a new way forward and Safeway was struggling to remain relevant and independent. Therefore, Kellogg were right to shake themselves down and equip themselves to compete more effectively going forward. They had launched snack bars and breakfast alternatives such as Rice Krispies Squares, Nutri-Grain and acquired Lender's Bagels, but internally I found the environment quite tough to settle into. There were clear divisions within the existing team between people embracing the change and those being dragged along reluctantly. The phrases 'new Kellogg' and 'old Kellogg' were bandied around as 'badges of (dis)honour' or used as 'weapons' in discussions. Ironically though, with the fresher eyes of someone new, it was typically the individuals I considered most 'old Kellogg' who'd swing the old Kellogg accusation like a scimitar to win a point or belittle someone with more flexibility and a more open mind. It was often quite demoralising to observe and difficult to redress.

Focusing on the future, the Sales Director was very forward thinking despite developing in the old Kellogg environment and really embraced the principle of personal development and investing in the team. Various training companies and coaches were engaged to support individual and team growth. To many this all seemed really eye opening and innovative and I certainly benefitted greatly from some of the training and introduction to concepts like Alpha Leadership and how 'vulnerability is power'. However, I don't consider that Kellogg's were really ready as an organisation to embrace some of the more radical or esoteric concepts at this time. I had some great experiences, worked on some great brands and met some very talented people at Kellogg's (although most moved on from the business quite quickly) but I never truly felt a great sense of belonging over my five years there.

The What Counts Factor

I have had thousands of pounds invested in my training and development by various companies which I really appreciate. My career has taken me to some wonderful places, meeting incredible people and having some amazing experiences however, I'd always emphasis that it's the culmination of little or everyday things that count and are the most effective way of building a true sense of belonging.

POINTS TO PONDER

- Things that cost little time or money and often get overlooked, can have a significant impact on those you lead and those who work around you.
- Consideration, support and respecting others usually costs nothing.
- Never underestimate the 'Power of the Pizza'! (or the Donut)
- Listen carefully. Remember what people say and if you can, identify their 'Baked Alaska'.

CHAPTER 5 – BEWARE OF THE BULL

For most people to progress in life and their career, confidence is crucial. The ability to back one's self and have faith in your own ability drives people to the top levels of achievement. However, some can struggle to differentiate between confidence and arrogance.

Francis Bacon wrote that "knowledge is power", though of course this was written long before the communication age and the internet. To some, throughout their career having access to all the data and "holding all the aces" is what provides the fuel for their self-confidence. Early in my career I was introduced to that idea that performance is a function of Knowledge plus Skills plus the right Attitude. Knowledge still comes at a price but access to it is now more readily available than for past generations. The videos on Youtube 'Shift Happens/Did You Know?' have been regularly updated from when I first saw it with even more incredible statistics about the amount of data generated around the world. In any meeting or discussion, the modus operandi of some is to know more than everyone else and continually drop in pertinent facts or updated information to show they are always in control.

One concern with this behaviour is when they don't know the answer. Some may become hesitant, bluster, and feel vulnerable as they are unsure how to proceed. Some will recognise that they don't know and accept their exposure. Unfortunately, a minority will ride their reputation as 'all seeing and all knowing' to elaborate and even make things up as they go along. I have seen this happen regularly and depending on the circumstances and company they are with, many are taken in. If the figure is authoritative and uber-confident most would not be prepared to challenge them. For a while, even to their superiors they can get away with it because they will 'romance' with such conviction. Eventually though, people get wise to it and the individual's credibility starts to be undermined. Being able to tell a story or paint a picture is an important part of leadership but tell a similar story too many times to the same audience and you will lose impact.

Aside from decisions being made on flawed data, the other issue is the example this sets. Those working for them can start to mimic this behaviour and without having the necessary character, experience or emotional intelligence can slip easily into arrogance, harming themselves and others.

In *Mind Games,* Neville Southall makes a telling observation that "there are too many people doing jobs in which they have to pretend to be experts on subjects that they don't know enough about, and that leads to people leading others without the best tools to help them succeed".

"It isn't you"

Eighteen months or so after joining Kellogg's the MD moved on to a new role in the US. His replacement was an external appointment and while we were waiting for him to start the Sales Director who had recruited me was also reassigned. In a meeting with the new MD to present our plans for the following year I made a comment that "when we get a new Sales Director, whoever that may be…" The MD quipped back "well I can tell you it isn't you". I was qualified for the position and though I didn't really expect it, the MD's comment was a bit cheap and embarrassing. A few people joked with me about it later.

I then decided to book some time with the MD and ask for his feedback on *why* it wasn't going to be me and what I should do to be ready when the role came up again. His feedback was vague though he did suggest that a powerful tactic was to "behave as if you are already in the position above". The person who we expected to get appointed, did indeed get the role and had repeatedly used that tactic which created a lack of trust and other issues within our peer group. Clearly there was evidence that this type of behaviour could work but it just wasn't an approach I was at all comfortable with. I viewed it as somewhat contrived advice, a bit disingenuous and undermined. The MD was only in role for about six months and his only legacy was a few other inappropriate comments and nothing of real substance.

Credibility

Equally as damaging as arrogance can be the impact on an individual's credibility when it all goes wrong. After identifying a real need for improved selling skills across AG Barr myself and a colleague developed and facilitated a bespoke sales training course which we piloted with my direct reports, all senior and experienced sales managers. The pre-work for the training was a Case Study requiring the trainees to produce a sales presentation which was sent in before the course. The idea was to share them with the group anonymously during the training, inviting feedback and critique. Whilst reviewing the presentations I had a feeling of déjà vu that I'd already seen one of the documents. On close inspection, the content of two of the presentations was about 85% the same, but pictures and graphs on one had been moved up and down and left to right to make it look different. I had not seen such a blatant example of copying homework since High School.

When the presentations were pinned up for all to see in the critique session on the day, I could detect murmurings of incredulity that two were so alike. The team worked out for themselves what had happened, and one person's credibility was clearly 'shot'. The person whose work had been copied was of course, very angry and explained to me that one of their colleagues had asked for some guidance and they had shared their presentation to help them get started. After waiting for the culprit to come clean, I eventually confronted them in private a week or so later. I could not believe that they tried to brazen it out, indignantly denying the clear plagiarism. They left the company of their own volition not long afterwards.

Fairy Tales are usually considered when thinking of children but, I have often used examples with the teams I have led as there are great teachings within them. Think of Rumpelstiltskin. The story ends well enough when he melts into a tantrum when his name is revealed. But why was the Miller's daughter put into that terrifying and threatening ordeal? It was because her father had 'bull shitted' to the King about her abilities and been called out! Similarly, in an iconic episode of Only Fools and Horses, Del Boy secures a contract to renovate a huge chandelier in a stately home. Attempting to be accepted in higher social circles and pretending to be someone he wasn't, he makes claims that he patently doesn't have the skills or resources to deliver against. As ever, Rodney, his younger brother calls him out, ridiculing Del by asserting that he can't restore the chandelier with "Superglue and Windowlene". Initially of course, just like the experienced manager on my sales course, Del brazens it all out, though when Rodney is out of earshot, he asks Grandad if they have any "Superglue and Windowlene"! It is true comedy and carries a pertinent lesson for business.

Impostor Syndrome

Although grocery wholesale is often regarded as a male dominated environment it has been refreshing to see the emergence of more and more female leaders. As most of AG Barr's Business Team Managers in wholesale were female, I joined them in attending the 2018 Women in Wholesale Conference where I witnessed a very powerful presentation from Hazel Detsiny, another Procter & Gamble alumni who has progressed to senior and influential positions at Unilever. Hazel talked about the concept and reality of Impostor Syndrome. For someone in her position as an MD to talk openly about this was inspiring and refreshing.

Impostor Syndrome is a psychological pattern in which one doubts one's accomplishments and has a persistent internalized fear of being exposed as a 'fraud'. It can be what drives 'bluster' and bullish behaviours or it can simply gnaw away and undermine one's confidence. Early research focused on prevalence among high-achieving women, though Impostor Syndrome has been recognized to affect both men and women equally. It takes courage and honesty to admit to these feelings, certainly in a 'data is powe'r type culture.

Contemporary thinking has moved on from Francis Bacon, with the concept that 'vulnerability is power'. If someone has a resolute and innate level of self-confidence, they are comfortable saying that they don't know or understand something and inviting those with more knowledge or understanding to enlighten them. One CEO I worked with had a highly effective way of occasionally holding out his hands palms upwards and saying "I'm not the expert here" thus inviting the experts to contribute more and lead to a solution. It takes true strength and courage to allow yourself to be vulnerable.

Again, I like the straightforward way Neville Southall expresses his thoughts here: "I know what I don't know. I don't have all the answers or even half of them. I know what I know and know how to use that to help myself and others, but I also know where my gaps are in knowledge and expertise. If you know what you don't know, it's far easier to be an open person than if you think you know everything"

POINTS TO PONDER

- Performance = Knowledge + Skills + Attitude.
- Confidence can be a key component of a positive attitude. But as Southall puts it, "confidence is having the faith in yourself that you'll learn from your mistakes, not that you won't make any"
- If you feel an on-set of Impostor Syndrome don't be too worried. It can affect any of us. It is how you deal with it that matters
- Be mature, considered, honest and avoid the bull(shit).

CHAPTER 6 – POO, PEE & PERIODS

An immature title for a chapter about maturity.

RBM

At one of my earliest sales launch meetings the presenter stood up and began to share details of a crucial brand initiative. All of the recent graduate sales intake sat together, and we were looking at each other bemused as the presenter kept referring to 'RBM'. Eventually someone had the courage to put their hand up (it wasn't me) and ask what it stood for. The answer "Runny Bowel Matter" was received to a chorus of giggles until the presenter told everyone to "stop laughing it makes us millions of profit". The brand was Pampers and we were all issued with product demonstration kits to simulate soiled nappies with our buying contacts.

If that took a maturity stretch to deal with, the worst was yet to come!

What is a Catamenial ?

There had been rumours that Procter & Gamble were going to launch into the Catamenial or Feminine Hygiene category. For those that do not know, think tampons and sanitary towels. These are absolutely crucial products for (females) a big proportion of the population, but not really items that most young males really want to be involved with. However, you learn to grow up, be mature and take your responsibilities seriously. I ended up working with those categories for several years and my maturity was accelerated, certainly in my professional life.

It was a touch embarrassing to take a silver attaché case into a meeting with a female buyer and open it to reveal knickers, sanitary towels, and vials of blue water to allow you to demonstrate absorbency of the product. However, there is a serious job to done and you are focused, determined and ambitious. In contrast, there was humiliating embarrassment when you forget to remove the said sampling kit from your car boot and 'the lads' discover it at the weekend!

One Friday afternoon sat at my desk I was working on various projects including the launch of new Always Pantyliners (whose USP reflected that they contained zeolite crystals). My mind was starting to wander towards the weekend, but I was suddenly snapped back to reality and could not quite believe what was written in a document I was studying. One of the reasons Procter & Gamble became one of the most successful businesses on the planet was their commitment to research & development and their deep understanding of consumers. Nothing in Procter & Gamble is done on a whim or by chance – everything is thoroughly researched and analysed. You did sometimes see a detached clinical logic lacking a touch 0f common sense though!

In the document, there was a graph headed 'Sniff Tests on Used Pantyliners'!

All manner of unpleasant thoughts came to mind, as my maturity temporarily regressed, especially at the thought of who actually conducted these tests? Eventually I found out that they were done in Italy, sometimes by experienced wine tasters who had a sense of smell attuned to delicate aromas in the wine! For the record, the zeolite crystals' role was to absorb odours and before I used the graph in the sales presentation, I added a touch of pragmatism and changed the title to 'Odour Emittance Analysis'.

MBW

By the time I was introduced to MBW, I had matured sufficiently to just get on with the project without silliness or histrionics. MBW stands for mild bladder weakness and the product, Certina, was targeted at females with occasional incontinence. Prevention of MBW is one of the reasons pregnant women are encouraged to perform regular pelvic floor exercises. As ever, comprehensive research had identified a consumer need and with their expertise in nappies and sanitary towels, Procter & Gamble had the necessary manufacturing experience. My role was to set up a test market in Aberdeen by securing the participation of the key retailers and monitoring product sales as the marketeers tested various communication methods. The TV advert was shown in the Grampian region and was typical Procter & Gamble—highlight a need and provide a solution. It showed a woman encountering the discomfort and embarrassment of MBW when sneezing and laughing, but new Certina was the perfect discrete answer.

I was ultimately relieved to hand over responsibility for nappies, feminine hygiene and MBW to someone who one day would become my boss in another company.

A day in the shit.

It would be difficult to tally how many days I've spent on training courses in various hotels and conference facilities. However, one day at an advertising agency in London will always stand out from my time in the marketing of cereals at Kellogg's. We had a project to look at introducing pre-biotics to products to improve gut health and spent literally all day being educated about poo and wind. There were some quite incredible facts on the day about litres of wind per day and weights of stools. The only other time I have witnessed as much fascination with body waste was when I drove my six-year-old son and a few pals to a birthday party – for some reason that was all they talked about in the car.

Having been required to grow up and mature so early in my career I struggled to find one advertising campaign in AG Barr as amusing as most of my peers did. IRN-BRU ran a campaign centred on the premise 'IRN-BRU gets you through' with one of the television executions showing a dad whose wife and mother-in-law want to call their new baby daughter Fanny, needing IRN-BRU to help him come to terms with it. Whilst I appreciated the advert, which was well received by the target audience, I wasn't particularly enamoured by grown men tittering about ordering point of sale and brand support items such as 'fanny magnets' and 'fanny packs'. I had either grown up at last or lost my sense of humour. The former I'd like to think.

The majority of people have careers where poo, pee and periods will never even be discussed in the work environment, so what other lessons can be learnt about maturity?

Personal Winning Strategy

As we go through our careers we develop, often subconsciously, a 'Personal Winning Strategy' that has helped us to progress. It is a collection of behaviours, actions, values and attitudes that have delivered our success and to an extent define who we are. Some people remain satisfied with this style and approach. There is nothing wrong with that, though there is a danger that as the world changes around you, your effectiveness may diminish. A style that has always delivered positive results may become less productive. What historically helped your career and development can start to hinder it. In some cases, this can develop to bitterness and resentment as others move onwards and upwards if the person isn't self-aware of the choice they've effectively made. This was captured in 2007 by Marshall Goldsmith when he published *What Got You Here Won't Get You There.*

Some adapt and modify their style covertly whilst others may make much more overt changes following training courses, feedback, and coaching. When someone makes a conscious, overt choice to change it can prove difficult and artificial. It can reduce trust and credibility as the sincerity of the individual is questioned. It creates a 'credibility gap'. For example :

"After going on that course, he now keeps coming to see me all the time"

"She must have been given some feedback because she's suddenly more friendly and polite"

"Their boss told them to change how they behave"

Others occasionally take this further and try to completely re-invent themselves. One person I worked with took great kudos from being known by their nickname early in the career. However, as they started to appreciate their own ability and their ambition grew, they realised the nickname was an inhibitor and suddenly started to insist on being referred to by their first name, correcting others in the process. They went from being fun loving, gregarious and affable to suddenly behaving far more considered, serious, and introverted. It was not me, and I'd relate the story personally if it were, but for ease let's just say that 'Smudger' tried to become Steven overnight. This caused a degree of suspicion and even ridicule with people referencing Prince, the pop star and musician who became The Artist Formerly Known as Prince'. Steven was talented and went on to have a really successful career, though the metamorphosis was only complete once he'd left the company and the moniker 'Smudger' completely behind.

In his book *The Cold War*, John Lewis Gaddis describes how the Americans with so much respect for their coveted constitution, initially found themselves concerningly disadvantaged against the Soviet Union. They viewed the Soviets as scorning theirAmerican values of truth, honour, justice, consideration for others and liberty for all. The Cold War transformed some American leaders into Machiavellians who resolved to "learn to be able to not be good" themselves and use this skill according to necessity. The pressure to act tougher or be more assertive and aggressive can become a real burden on someone who fundamentally is not equipped to act in such a way. The CIA might have eventually relished the challenge in covert international operations deemed for the greater good, but in a business environment, people trying to be something they are not rarely succeeds in my experience.

One of the brightest, most considerate, and supportive people I worked with sometimes fell into this trap. In order to succeed and gain more respect they believed that they should consciously act more assertively and authoritatively however, this served to undermine their credibility. In a round of 360 feedback they were upset when someone suggested they should "stop acting like a captain of industry". What they needed was some better coaching and feedback to make them more confident and effective with the unique skill set they had.

Consistency is key

Youthful energy and experience boost confidence as you start a career journey and then maturity and experience provide more confidence later. It is the long time in between that many struggle with as they seek to understand who they are, what they enjoy and ultimately what level of progress is realistic (and some are never mature enough to see that).

In my early days at Procter & Gamble we went on a lot of in-house training courses, usually moderated by more experienced and senior managers. Given the high-potential, competitive graduates that joined Procter & Gamble, the beginning of these courses was a bit like the start of a Grand Prix where everyone scrabbled to be in front at the first corner. Their relative immaturity, combined with naked ambition created a high-octane training cocktail. Each wanted to be recognised as the leader within their peer group by the senior figures who could support and accelerate their career. It makes sense, but personally I hated it and would withdraw into my shell a little until there was a more appropriate opportunity to shine.

Some lack the maturity to realise that the strongest leaders don't always need to lead overtly. They almost become addicted to being the leader. They can't help themselves, as they have an irresistible compulsion to lead and manage in every situation, within their own function and beyond. Whether it is general business planning, operational meetings or choice of pub or restaurant for dinner (or tea!!) they stride off in front like Peter Pan and expect everyone to sing "Following the Leader, the Leader, the Leader".

Two particular problems can arise from this. Firstly, they might not actually be as clever as they think and go in the wrong direction. Also, even when they are correct, it does not help others to learn and develop if they are always deprived of an opportunity to lead for themselves.

In a career it is being competitive, consistent and considerate over the long term that earns respect and cements leadership, not fighting for attention at the start.

POINTS TO PONDER

- We all grow, develop and mature during our careers.
- Our personal winning strategies should adapt and evolve covertly to ensure continued growth.
- Overtly reinventing yourself or adopting an alien style can create distrust and credibility gaps. This should be avoided.
- Be yourself, be mature and be "comfortable in your own skin".

CHAPTER 7 – THE ILLUMINATI

Don't worry, this section will not be investigating David Icke, Reptilian Super Beings or the Protocols of the Elders of Zion. It's not an assessment of corporate conspiracy theories (though Procter & Gamble attracted rumours of satanic links at one time, primarily due to their moon and stars logo) but more an opportunity to highlight two words of fundamental importance to those seeking to develop high performing teams or build modern progressive cultures.

Decision making

It is important too to refence that there will always be a need for hierarchical decision making in large organisations. Procter & Gamble had a training program called Decision Mapping. The basic concept being that business decisions require a combination of various evaluators to help determine costs and benefits of different options, any number of implementors to make things happen, but ultimately there is only one owner of the decision. In large organisations, people at various levels are empowered to make decisions of varying magnitude and be accountable for the consequences. However, the very biggest decisions will go right to the top with CEOs or chairpersons ultimately holding the casting vote in board meetings.

In a similar vein there is often a need for confidentiality on sensitive matters within organisations. This can be for legal reasons like 'insider trading' of stocks and shares when some officers have access to important results ahead of the market or propriety knowledge and data of value to competitors. Again, board members have clear responsibilities which is why in the autumn of 2012 when we arrived at our desks in AG Barr one morning we were greeted by a hastily written e:mail explaining that AG Barr and Britvic plc were in advanced stages of a merger. Few outside AG Barr's and Britvic's plc boards knew about the discussions so it was a big surprise and had to be briefed to employees prematurely as a newspaper had obtained some details and gone to print. This would have been a major development in the UK grocery and soft drinks markets, though ultimately it did not come to pass. It is an interesting story as to why it did not happen, though best told by those closer to proceedings.

So, acknowledging some of the limitations underpinning decision making and confidentiality, two 'T' words are crucial in the way many organisations aspire to operate.

TRUST and TRANSPARENCY.

(N.B. there is a four letter expletive with two 'T's that occasionally gets used when there is a lack of the above and I have heard this used to describe several individuals during my career!).

I was particularly engaged on one Leadership Programme, where we were introduced to Patrick Lencioni's Five Dysfunctions of a Team model. I would strongly recommend reading further material or watching videos of this on Youtube.

A degree of 'healthy tension' among people in an organisation can spark creativity and help to solve problems. According to the *HBR*, 'the absence of conflict is not harmony, it's apathy', therefore, you need sufficient levels of trust to channel any conflict constructively.

The basic emphasis on trust and the importance of vulnerability in Lencioni's work really struck a chord and I was greatly encouraged that at long last the way I'd always tried (consciously and sub-consciously) to treat people and go about my business was finally being lauded and recommended to my peers. I was in a quite paternalistic and 'knowledge is power' type culture and observed a mix of delight, disinterest and disdain across my senior management and director peer group.

A picturesque hotel on a glorious day was the perfect learning environment for this training and we were tasked with using cut up magazines and pictures to each build a collage representing Lencioni's ideas. And yes, we were getting paid whilst doing this! All manner of bizarre creations ensued, but the design most recognised and applauded was the large letter T that one attendee had produced. A simple and clear representation of Trust. The irony was, that the person who produced it was viewed as acting very 'Theory X' with their own team, closely micro-managing them and considered by many to lack trust in any judgement except their own.

People can also make some comical attempts to keep your trust after they have tested it. A client recently cancelled some work at very short notice. In their brief email, they expressed that "As a rule of thumb I don't normally let people down" – I immediately thought,

"Oh great, you've singled me out for poor treatment then!"

Psychological Safety

It is not always easy or wise to speak out, although it should be! I once shared a concern based on genuine observations in a management board meeting at head office. I expressed my worries that we had a growing morale issue, particularly across the other company locations.

The MD dismissed my suggestion as "bollocks" and the room went silent. Tumbleweed time. No peers supported my comments, even though I knew from individual discussions that several held similar views. When scores from the next employee engagement report came in, most crucial measures had indeed declined.

It may be referred to now as 'psychological safety' but this is not a new phenomenon—think about *The Emperor's New Clothes* again. They all knew he was naked, but it was only the naivety and inhibitions of a child that expressed the reality. People just didn't feel safe to speak up.

The Clique

It was at university where I first encountered the word clique. I lived in a fully catered Hall of Residence with over four hundred other students. Each year a President and other Officers were elected to form a Junior Common Room (JCR) Committee to effectively run student affairs for example social events, the private bar etc. However, new residents believed that aside from the JCR there was effectively a 'clique' of final year students who in reality were in charge. These were a relatively small mixed group who it was perceived, did not readily allow others to join them. I was elected President towards the end of my first year and found that the 'clique' weren't really a clique' at all – they were just a group of friends, in their final year who kept themselves to themselves a bit more to concentrate on their studies.

I engaged with them on several matters seeking their input and they were helpful and supportive, but the idea of a sinister, powerful, closed elite did stick in my mind, coming to the fore again through Dan Brown's books years later!

As mentioned, how transparent any organisation can be is a matter of debate. Some things have to be kept confidential and shared on a need to know basis, whilst other things can be discussed and shared more openly. I always tried to be as open as possible with my teams and give everyone input whenever I could. I have witnessed cliques forming and managers having a disproportionately close relationship with one or a couple in their team, and it wasn't healthy.

One of the sales directors I worked for had a clear 'favourite' and close confidant that made the rest of the leadership team regularly feel excluded. We would often be waiting for a meeting to start, the pair in question would arrive late or be seen to have a quick one to one outside the room and then various decisions or outcomes would be presented to the rest of us almost as a fait accompli – needless to say, the rest of us were demotivated, disengaged and dissatisfied by the lack of transparency.

Similarly, groups can often join a meeting to discuss alternative scenarios and make informed decisions. However, the boss, or a combination of the boss and their clique of closest confidantes, have already decided what is going to happen and the meeting becomes a sham. This lack of transparency and trust in the broader group leaves people feeling frustrated, isolated and insecure. Not a good culture.

I think of small, tight-knit groups who manage with a lack of trust and transparency as 'The Illuminati'. They form a small closed unit with a disingenuous level of influence on the proceedings of a department or function. Without openness they ultimately only trust themselves, stifling the development and career progression of others.

Again, this can be born of arrogance (I/we know best), or insecurity (the less who know the more I can control) or sometimes a complete lack of awareness. Whatever the reason, it does not build teamwork and Lencioni is right, trust needs to underpin everything.

"We need more honest discussion in business, less excessive politeness and politics."

Melanie Healey, Retiring Group President, P&G / Verizon Board of Directors

THINK LONG AND HARD ABOUT THE FOLLOWING:

- When Trust and Transparency are low, Cliques and T**ts can flourish!

CHAPTER 8 – CONFLICT

The second of Lencioni's team dysfunctions refers to the conflicts that can arise in organisations.

Relativity

In analysing conflict, you need to first consider what defines it and this will vary by individual and within organisations.

Many agree that a level of healthy tension within a business is valuable. It stimulates challenge and growth. It prevents too much 'group think' and resists complacency setting in.

Problems arise when one person's healthy tension is interpreted or perceived as aggression or conflict by others. I am not aware of any recognised standards or calibrated scales to measure this - it is very subjective.

Some people, for multiple reasons, just do not have the self-awareness to understand the 'impact versus intent' dynamic of their communication or behaviours and thereby create conflict. In direct comparison, others may be particularly sensitive, less able to deal with routine challenge or disagreement and perceive conflict that isn't really there. Like many things, we have a spectrum to consider.

In managing this, most effective teams accommodate a combination of personalities, skills, viewpoints and styles that create and thrive on the healthy tension. However, when you have that combination, there is also greater risk of conflict unless there is real trust within the team - Patrick Lencioni territory. If there is trust and strong leadership, both bullish and bearish tendencies can be accommodated and utilised for the greater good. Similarly, personality differences highlighted through profiling (e.g. DISC etc.) can be harnessed constructively and used to drive positive and productive output.

Internal versus External Conflict

My career has mostly been working in sales and outward-facing roles dealing directly with customers. I always found external conflict easier to handle than differences and disagreements in my own company. Why?

External conflict (i.e., with customers or other parties) tends to be quite overt. It is usually about financial matters or trading terms. Some people use conflict and exert pressure as negotiation tactics and whilst that can be challenging (and occasionally become personal) there is a clear and obvious reason for it - to get a strong result and satisfactory outcome. You may 'fall out' temporarily, but you typically move on once an acceptable agreement has been reached. The person you are dealing with externally has little direct influence on your career or reputation, especially if you secure an outcome that meets internal requirements. Whether there was conflict and how well you handled it is of little concern to anyone else (other than perhaps your boss or coach who should be there to help you improve).

Internal conflict of an unproductive nature or in an environment lacking trust can be much more covert and even sinister. It might just be that some people have different styles and 'rub each other up the wrong way' (e.g. in DISC profiling the D (dominant) and S (steadiness) display opposite characteristics). However, there can also be much more to it than that. The metaphor 'stabbed in the back' implies a manifestation of more considered political conflict, sometimes initially hidden and subtle, but culminating in betrayal in meetings, the boardroom or a whispering campaign about you.

Ego and the desire to be (or be perceived as) 'top dog' or leader can play a huge part, as can internal bias and prejudice. Sometimes, internal conflict can be driven by one personality. For example, people may have worked with the obstreperous individual who constantly seems to disagree, compulsively challenge everything and pick fights with anyone or everyone!

A Culture of Conflict

Developing a culture based on challenge (often leading to conflict) may be encouraged or even policy in some organisations. A colleague at Procter & Gamble once went for an interview at L'Oreal and was put off by, as they described it, the prevailing 'spirit of confrontation' that was heavily emphasised by the interviewer. Plans and ideas (and the person presenting them) were aggressively challenged to see if they would hold up, as opposed to the more supportive and nurturing environment that we had at P&G. Similarly, I know a few people who in the noughties worked in the Cauldwell Group, founded by British billionaire John Cauldwell. They were high calibre individuals, but their stays were brief as they couldn't settle into the high octane and at times quite 'brutal', aggressive environment.

Constructive criticism, even when it develops into a form of conflict can be a hugely powerful and positive tool but is a twin-edged sword that can be demotivational, destructive and damaging to an idea or an individual.

Taken to extremes, ongoing conflict can become bullying, which in days gone by was probably more tolerated in the workplace than in the more enlightened times we have now. Behaviours and comments quite common in the past would now be subject to a full-on HR enquiry. Nevertheless, damaging conflict still exists, though tolerance levels are thankfully lower.

As identified previously, conflict is a function of communication and some people will not take accountability for the consequences of what they say. If something isn't received positively and creates conflict, they make it all about the recipient and deflect responsibility. The following is a powerful quote, again from Neville Southall:

"Part of the problem is the blurred line between 'banter' and 'abuse' and the mistakes people make when drawing that line. All I hear now is that you can't say a word to anyone 'these days' for fear of causing offence or upsetting them, implying that nobody can take a joke. But that is simply not true. It just depends upon your relationship with them. The onus is on you to avoid offending, not on people to avoid being offended. The fault lies with you. Anything else is victim-blaming."

From Mind Games *by Neville Southall, former professional football (soccer) player and now social campaigner.*

What are the causes? Who creates the conflict?

One of the key things to identify when handling conflict is to find what is driving it.

Is it the obstreperous person who challenges for the sake of challenging, and if so, what causes them to do that?

It might be that it is someone with the knowledge and skills to perform well, but for some reason has an attitude that draws them towards a more challenging style resulting in continual conflict. It is probably the role of their manager or coach to try to understand and help them. It may be due to some insecurity or lack of self-confidence that makes them default to challenge everything.

Alternatively, it could be a deflection tactic as they lack sufficient knowledge and skills for their role but have an innate sense of superiority viewing 'attack as the best form of defence'. There are people who get to senior levels of organisations in this way, often leaving a divisive culture behind them. This is harder to coach and usually needs a senior and experienced third party to get the person to 'open up' on why they adopt this approach, before they can change.

Grievance or revenge can be a source of conflict. There are sometimes disgruntled individuals or groups of employees who seek to sabotage change and development. This particularly occurs when new people with different styles come into an organisation. I have personally experienced the difficulties caused by established individuals consciously rejecting and actively undermining the organisational, systems and cultural changes I was recruited to deliver.

It is important to try to understand the cause of this conflict and see if you can help and encourage a change in mindset. Some refuse to deviate from the path of conflict and quite often will ultimately leave. Many thrive, by embracing and adapting to positive change, whilst others become marginalised malcontents, simmering away in the background but mostly keeping their issues to themselves.

Conflict can also arise from a touch too much passion or enthusiasm. This is rarely a long-term problem and can be quickly overcome. If anything, it is a good problem to have. I have always said I would sooner have to rein in a team or individual than have to put my boot up their backside to get them going! If an over-zealous approach leads to some conflict, it usually falls more into the 'healthy tension' category described earlier.

One thing I have never subscribed to is when some managers or 'leaders' deliberately create conflict. This may be with a positive intent as a catalyst to spark creativity, but some even do it for their own amusement. (Hitler enjoyed having his acolytes squabbling for his favour!) I worked with someone whose team described how their boss would deliberately 'throw a hand grenade' into the team meetings because they liked to see what happened. Not a style I would support. Playing 'Devil's Advocate' and challenging ideas is constructive, but hand grenades were invented to hurt, maim and destroy. This seems more like a power game or ego trip than a way to build a team.

To be clear, I consider healthy tension to be constructive and very important. The 'Emperor's New Clothes' environment where everyone nods and won't say what is obvious is not the way forward. It leads to groupthink and stifles progress. Challenge is crucial but needs to avoid becoming conflict, remaining at a productive not destructive level.

Dealing with Conflict

The first step is to determine if conflict is driven by either behaviours *and* some principles or is genuinely just principle based.

If the former, there is less likelihood of satisfactory outcomes. It is best to either delay or even avoid the conflict by closing it down (in a group environment) and working with those causing the conflict separately and in private. Try to find out the cause or reasons for the behaviours and coach the person or group to refrain, emphasising the damage they are doing. If they won't, you may need to keep them out of situations where they can create issues while you work on a longer-term solution, possibly in tandem with HR.

When conflict is purely principle-driven, it is vital to have the views aired, discussed, and considered, even if all do not agree. So long as they *all commit* to a way forward you can move on. You can only get to this if there is a high degree of trust between individuals or within a team. Only with trust can you successfully resolve conflict and move through the subsequent stages of Lencioni's model.

Final Thought

TRUST is such an important word in business. If you think you have it, but really you haven't, you may end up being stabbed in the back!

POINTS TO PONDER

- Appreciate that there is a relativity to conflict and seek to take an objective view.
- Understand who and what factors are causing disagreement
- Determine whether the conflict is purely on principle or driven by behaviour, and respond accordingly.

CHAPTER 9 – PANDORA'S BOX

Motivation

The principles of leading, managing and motivating others run right through this book. A few simple ideas have helped me manage the motivation and development of individuals in the teams I have managed. No complex psychological theories or models, just some basic guidelines:

- Listen to your people.
- Know them, understand them and encourage them.
- Celebrate their skills and successes
- Draw learning from their setbacks.
- Support their development needs.

As Aleksandr from advertising (Compare the) Meerkat would say, 'Simples'.

Networking

"If you want to get ahead, get a set of clubs" was some advice given to me early in my Procter & Gamble career after I'd told a colleague that I didn't play golf. The person giving the advice had only been in the business a year or so longer but had clearly got to grips with the cultural 'game that had to be played. To be fair, they went on to have a very successful career reaching the highest levels in one of the biggest global FMCG companies, so early appreciation of the power of networking really paid off.

Of course, building relationships that matter within your own organisation and externally is extremely important for a successful company and a blossoming career. It's the terminology that often causes discomfort. Building a broad and effective personal network requires a blend of personality, charisma and interpersonal skills. However, when network was used as a verb in the FMCG world it suggested a more cynical, exploitative and obsequious approach.

Whilst I have always been able to make friends and find connections with people, I'd typically say I wasn't a very good 'networker' in a business sense. I always feel a little disingenuous approaching someone because of what their role and position might be able to do for me, as opposed to who they are as a person. For others small talk and making contacts is an innate skill. I have witnessed some smooth, effective operators, completely at ease with CEOs or the security person at the entrance. For me though, building effective networks takes time, requires a degree of familiarity and trust. If the relationship you develop isn't genuinely robust, resilient and reciprocal, you can fall open to the accusation of merely being a 'namedropper'.

Networking away from FMCG opened my eyes though. In the small to medium enterprise (SME) environment, it is a more facilitated and enjoyable activity. The events run by organisations like regional Chambers of Commerce, local business clubs and Business Network International (BNI) have been set up by like-minded people with like-minded objectives. They are structured and open to people developing referral partners and clients, rather than jostling with a hundred other suppliers for a minute in front of a buying director or CEO.

I enjoy the business breakfasts and networking sessions facilitated through my membership of St Helens, Halton and Greater Manchester Chambers. There are dedicated people there who are focused on championing their local business communities and providing valuable support to the local economy and business ecosystem.

BNI tends to create polarised views due to how structured and orderly the events and meetings are. It is a truly global organisation with a great emphasis on training and personal development. I was impressed when on one of the training webinars the Procter & Gamble origin story was referred to. People tend to either love BNI or recoil from it. From my perspective, the chapter I engaged with had some great characters and successful people, however, I have committed my time to more local groups like Real 5 St Helens and the Orion Marketing Group in Wigan.

Know, Like, Trust

This is a phrase I have heard a lot in SME circles, though I've tended to summarise this through my career as the notions of *like* versus *respect*

The people you tend to admire the most are the ones you like AND respect.

Some you may respect due to their technical skills, performance, results etc., but you might not like them that much. Their style may be very different from your own.

Then there are people you like, whose company you might enjoy, but you don't always respect some of the things they do or their approach to certain situations.

Finally, at the bottom of the list are the people you neither like nor respect and you tend to avoid.

We meet and interact with a variety of people and sometimes how you view them changes for better or worse once you get to know them more. The biggest disappointment tends to be when someone's actions and behaviours, or a group you have liked and respected, starts to erode those feelings. It has happened to me a few times with senior people I've looked up to, or a group I've been part of, behaving in a way that resulted in me feeling a little duped, or even betrayed.

Meetings

During most business careers we spend a huge amount of our time in meetings of one form or another. Some are stimulating and enjoyable, while in others you can tell that most people would rather be somewhere else. Managing effective meetings is a skill that whole books have been written about and of course in 2020 pretty much the whole business community utilised virtual meetings. Many salespeople, in particular, were already familiar with Microsoft Teams and Google Hangouts but for many, Zooming was a new experience.

I shared the following guidance with my team a long time ago, so long ago that I can't remember who to credit for some of the source material.

Whatever type of meeting you're leading, whether it's in-person or virtual, you'll have a better chance of being successful when the participants follow some general protocols and agree on the 'rules'.

Some rules are established and documented, while others simply constitute good manners. For example, if you're asked to attend a meeting, you acknowledge whether or not you'll be attending. You review the agenda. You arrive on time. If it's necessary to leave the meeting early, you let the leader know.

Most who attend meetings know that someone - usually the meeting leader - manages the agenda and time. Notes are taken during the meeting and distributed after. Participants don't 'talk over' one another, and when someone makes a comment, it's appropriate to acknowledge that it was heard, whether you agree with what was said or not.

In many companies, it's an acceptable protocol for a participant to call attention to time or agenda issues if the facilitator doesn't. When a subject occurs that is unrelated to the agenda or takes the meeting off course, participants generally agree that a 'car park' can be used to capture these for later discussion. Participants in virtual meetings generally agree background noises are disruptive. This includes multi-processing such as checking emails or filing during the meeting. Whatever rules you establish for your meetings, make sure they promote the following:

Equality - This prevents one or two people from dominating a meeting and preventing others from having the opportunity to speak. People must respect one another's opinions and ideas and allow them the chance to voice them.

Harmony - Participants should not have to raise their voices or argue to be heard. When there are set rules as to when people may speak, you attain better harmony.

Efficiency - If there are fewer problems during your meetings, you won't waste time managing difficulties. Instead of spending time trying to get your meetings under control, you can spend it on accomplishing your objective.

It's important to establish ground rules. They'll help promote equality, harmony, and efficiency. They also provide a reference should issues occur later. If, for example, a participant is preventing others from speaking, it's appropriate to refer to the ground rules and remind participants that they agreed to allow everyone to speak.

This all sounds a bit formal but doesn't have to be. With trust, transparency and appropriate respect for others, a meeting can flow.

Digging

On many occasions I have dealt with people who behave as if every situation has a right or wrong outcome and of course, they are always right! Whether such absolute conviction stems from arrogance or insecurity varies with the individual but doesn't tend to be helpful, either with peers or in a position of authority. What is even worse is if that person 'sticks' resolutely to 'their guns', becomes overly defensive and develops an entrenched position. Having dug themselves into a hole, they just keep on digging! A little bit of humility and a few acts of contrition often have a positive effect.

The Miners Lamp

The analogy here is a tendency for some managers to operate wearing a miner's lamp on their head, which identifies and isolates both certain projects and/or certain individuals under an intense light, but leaves others in the dark, neglected. This can impact morale and motivation negatively and inhibit progress in other areas. Whilst some projects are of shorter duration, other projects end up viewed as flavour of the month or a manager's 'hobbyhorse' – they then move on, but the people who have invested a lot of time and effort feel forgotten or confused. In people management terms the phrase 'blue eyed boy' or 'teacher's pet' is used by overlooked or resentful colleagues. When managers are perceived to have favourites, who are always engaged first to help with pressing issues or an on-going priority (ie. where the miner's light is shining) they may be considered unfairly 'elevated' in status. This can cause a degree of friction with their colleagues, but can also leave the individual a little insecure when they are not receiving as much attention.

Walk the Talk

This is a phrase I have heard often and it's all about commitment and being intentional in your thoughts and actions or 'doing what you say you'll do' to put it in simpler terms. In all walks of life, you encounter many people who talk the talk but don't actually walk the walk. This happens at all levels in organisations but is probably most damaging when senior figures neglect to lead by example. Actions often speak louder than words.

When all of Kellogg's senior managers were invited to attend *Thinking Outside the Box* training (a sizeable investment), the day started with the MD spending five minutes extolling the virtues of the training and how important it was to the future of the business. Then he promptly disappeared and wasn't seen again across the two days!

We also had training when I was in the Marketing team centred around the idea of *Mi Casa, Tu Casa* (Your House, My House) and the importance of trying so see and understand things from another person's perspective. The training was good and made a lot of sense. However, in a meeting not long after, I asked the marketing director who had commissioned the training to see if he could try to consider something from my perspective. He flatly refused! So much for the £20,000 training! So much for .walking the talk'.

The Leadership Programme in my latter days at Barr included all the department heads from the management board, plus various other senior managers, the CEO and executive directors who remained for the duration of the course. Whilst there might have been the odd suggestion and scepticism and a few obsequious remarks from those looking to impress, by attending the full program, and participating fully the directors provided a great example of 'walking the talk'.

The first time I heard the phrase be 'tough on the problem, not the people' was in respect to Tesco and I think the sentiment here is spot on. I have never worked for Tesco, so whether this mantra is adhered to internally I don't know. Unfortunately, I have experienced situations across most of the key grocery retailers and occasionally in wholesale, when the sentiment has been distorted and pressure has been directed personally rather than on fixing a problem.

Self-Perception

Some of the personality profiles and psychometric testing I've experienced address the differences between self-perception (i.e. how you see yourself) and how others see or perceive you. I am far from an expert in decoding all the data from the various tools and profiles used, so my observations here are brief.

One thing that does strike me is that some get really 'hung up' on the word perception and the phrase 'perception is reality'. Of course, we all make judgements and observations on how we perceive people and situations ourselves and as humans we all make mistakes. For example, I have heard many variations around the theme of "I never really liked him, but once you get to know him, he's really sound" illustrates how we can get things wrong. However, during my career, the people who I have witnessed be most frustrated by the word perception tend to be those with lower self-awareness and less propensity to be honest with themselves. Net result, self-perception and others perception are misaligned!

Self-Proclaimed

In a similar vein I have always been wary of those prone to self-proclamation. Of course, some are considered experts in their field and really are, but its typically others who bestow this title on them. If you are going to describe yourself as an expert in something, you had really better be one! This idea does tend to rub against the grain in business. Just look at Linkedin profiles (including my own!) where most of us feel the need to sell ourselves. One person I worked with for many years often referred to their own high levels of integrity and honest approach, effectively using these statements like a challenge. I found this uncomfortable and passive aggressive behaviour as they were almost daring you to challenge them. I had several altercations with this person regarding honesty and integrity. However, as this type of person will rarely make admissions, you have to have incontrovertible evidence to 'call them out'.

Recruitment & Interviewing

I have interviewed hundreds of people through my career and it is typically an activity I enjoy. Sometimes you are won over by a person as soon as they enter the room whilst others you warm to and the liking gets stronger as the interview progresses. On occasion you realise straight away that they should never have been called in to begin with!

Companies have different recruitment and interviewing strategies and the process continues to evolve through on-line screening, profiling, interviews on Zoom and now AI interviews effectively conducted by robots when you are asked questions by a pre-filmed interviewer. However, I still hold to the adage that people do business with people. We possess emotions and instincts which we need to keep using.

The person who doesn't bother to turn up for an interview (as opposed to the person you occasionally come across who is there in 'body but not mind') is always a frustration and usually the result of bad planning or bad manners. There is also a flip side to this coin though. I was never particularly comfortable with the idea of just benchmarking external candidates with your own personnel. In terms of comparing abilities when appointing someone to an actual role, then fair enough. However, I have experienced both scenarios where a company 'benchmarks' to 'see what's out there' with no real intention to recruit or just to legitimise a preferred internal appointment. This is not a transparent activity and borders on arrogance when wasting individuals' time.

Second Chance Saloon

Some of the world's great organisations have had policies that once you have left, you can't come back. This was certainly the belief when I was at Procter & Gamble. When I did hand my notice in, it was primarily for geographical reasons. I had just got married, we had our first child on the horizon and so I wanted to stay in the northwest. The Sales Vice President was understanding, though disappointed and said some words that I have always appreciated. He said that in all his years with the company he'd only ever met one person with such a strong geographical attachment as myself and said that if things didn't work out with my move to Kellogg's, I should contact him and he'd find a way to re-employ me. It was hard leaving such a first-class operation as Procter & Gamble and hearing those words made it even harder. I had looked to leave a few years before and was persuaded to stay – one of the best decisions I ever made, but this time was different, and I needed to move on.

Since then, I have always been prepared to let good people come back into the team. For some it is an ego issue in not wanting to let someone return. When I was making such decisions at AG Barr, I was purely focused on getting the best possible person for the job. If we did not have an appropriate candidate internally, I would recruit outside and on several occasions that meant the return of a 'prodigal'. We all make mistakes, and my view is that if a good operator has realised that the grass wasn't actually greener on the other side, they could hit the ground running on their return and their gratitude would probably make them even more committed than previously. Clearly, you would not take *anyone* back, but why penalise the person and the organisation if they were effective, popular and could add value?

If someone you know is a strong performer and they describe what you've built as "a work culture with high trust levels, where everyone is valued" and then admit they "knew from the moment I left that no other business can replicate this" and finally offers that they are "extremely grateful for the chance to come back and I really do owe you much more than a pint or two" – wouldn't you be pleased to welcome them back?

The Beliefs of Excellence

For twenty or so years, I have often referred to the *Beliefs of Excellence* by Cecara Consulting, introduced during my time with Kellogg's. Simple ideas providing resolute guidance.

- Everyone is unique.
- Everyone makes the best possible choice available to them at the time.

- There is no failure, only feedback.
- Behind every behaviour is a positive intention.
- The meaning of the communication is the response that you get.
- Mind and body are part of the same system.
- The person with the most flexibility in thinking and behaviour stands the best chance of success.

Yes, some of the beliefs can at times be difficult to accept in certain scenarios or with certain individuals however, I have found them a great way to help me understand and appreciate things I haven't readily agreed with.

POINTS TO PONDER

- Build and utilise an effective network, but be wary of 'name dropping'
- "If you want to get ahead, get a set of clubs" – to be fair, this *can* help!
- Being liked and respected is a wonderful position to attain but remember the responsibility you carry. People feel duped and even betrayed if your standards slip.
- If you wear a Miners Lamp, widen the beam.
- Walk the Talk.
- Commendations, complements, and positive feedback are infinitely more valuable when they come from others, not yourself
- If a talented, sincere, and honest individual makes a mistake in leaving, why not let the prodigal return?

"Many, many thanks from all at Booker for the contribution you have made to our business with AG Barr. You will be a big loss though we look forward to working with you in the future and if we can help, just shout. All the very best, Charles and all your friends at Booker."

Charles Wilson, CEO Booker Wholesale.

"Thank-you for all your help. We've had a strong relationship with AG Barr and whilst we have not always seen eye to eye or gained agreement, the business has moved forward considerably and always outstripped growth of many larger suppliers with considerably more resources available. You were never afraid of tension and always had customers and the Barr business at the heart of everything you did. Talent skill and experience still count."

David Beardmore, Packaged Food/BWS & Tesco Brand Director.

"Your leaving is a real shame to hear as you were doing a great job working with us"

Dawood Pervez, Managing Director Bestway Wholesale.

"You've been always been a voice of reason and you're one of the good guys in the industry who knows it inside out"

John C Baines, Trading Director Unitas Wholesale.

CHAPTER 10 – STRATEGY AND TACTICS

Strategy is the second prominent business word that I would often ask interviewees to define (the first being leadership). Answers would vary appreciably, and this is an area where scholars, analysts and others have spent a good deal more time in understanding than I have. I would never describe myself as a 'grand strategist' and at Procter & Gamble my personal development feedback often said I needed to demonstrate improved strategic thinking.

Ironically on arrival at Kellogg's I was soon advised that I needed to focus less on strategy and "roll my sleeves up more" to get things done!

On one occasion, Carlos Gutierrez the CEO was over from the Battle Creek, Michigan, Head Office for a management conference at the Broadwater Hall in Manchester. When it came to the question and answer session the usual array of questions (e.g. "If you could wave a magic wand to change anything in the business what would it be?", "How important is NPD?" etc) were asked. Then someone asked Carlos about his strategy for long term growth in the share price and company valuation. The answer was interesting – "if we keep hitting our sales numbers on a quarterly basis, investors will have confidence in our stock, and it will continue to rise". This simple, short-term response took many by surprise when they were expecting some grandiose, intellectualised formula for growth.

In AG Barr, I consistently achieved, under pressure, the short term deliverables (with customers) to hit the performance required in a UK plc, to then invariably get feedback in my appraisal suggesting that I needed to look to expand my strategic thinking and focus farther ahead! Confused? Yes, so was I at times!

I have seen strategy defined in various ways. One simple description is that strategy is the effort to align external opportunity with internal capability. Procter & Gamble suggested that strategy was the choices made to beat competition over the long term. They developed the cascading OGSM Model (Objectives, Goals, Strategies and Measures) which is an excellent, logical framework though I rarely found that people had the time and inclination to rigorously ensure its update and intellectual integrity. I have since seen OGSM deployed elsewhere in adapted and diluted forms.

At one conference, Mark Price (now Lord Price) made a presentation about strategy. He discussed the strategic effectiveness of doing the opposite of your competitors. So, when Tesco, Sainsbury etc were pushing points based, delayed benefit Loyalty Card schemes, Waitrose offered their card holders a free coffee in their cafe on every store visit instead. This was incredibly successful in attracting customers to the stores, so much so, that they eventually had to change it due to exploitation from 'free loaders'!

Top businesses seek to recruit the brightest minds however, Lord Price's observation is often overlooked as a 'monkey see, monkey do' response to competitors' actions can take over. Early in the nineties Procter & Gamble and Unilever had both looked to reduce packaging and save costs on laundry projects by introducing plastic pouches to refill soap powder boxes. Procter & Gamble picked up some intelligence that Lever Brothers had placed an order for literally hundreds of thousands of rectangular tin boxes. Putting two and two together they realised what Lever were probably trying to do. They sought an alternative supplier and ordered biscuit type tins branded as Ariel, Fairy, Daz and Bold and then sold them containing a refill pouch of the respective brand of powder. I honestly can't remember who got to shelf first, but the market was awash with them for months!

On a couple of occasions at AG Barr we resisted the urge to just copy our rivals. Firstly, when concentrated Energy Shots were launched by Relentless, Red Bull and a few other brands. Rockstar had these products in the US and wanted to launch however, the AG Barr view was that they were mot really soft drinks and declined. When Britvic launched Robinson's Squash'd small bottles of super concentrate for squash on the go, Vimto and some others followed suit. AG Barr were a minor player in the cordials and dilutes market though there were suggestions from that we should launch something similar under the Simply brand. We didn't. Fortunately, common sense prevailed as it is fair to say that both Energy Shots and 'Squash'd' products burned dimly and briefly and could not be considered a success.

Boost Drinks have maintained a clear strategy that contrasts with most of their competitors in Energy Drinks. They chose to only supply the wholesale and independent channels, electing to not seek distribution for their products in the national grocery retailers. This approach has made them really relevant to the customers they do work with and led to incredibly strong close relationships. Whilst securing listings for their products in supermarkets could massively increase their volumes, Boost continue to operate to a strict, disciplined and successful strategy.

In the twilight of my career at AG Barr the Soft Drinks Sugar Levy was announced and came into force in April 2018. There were two distinct strategies deployed: Coca-Cola, Britvic (Pepsi) and Red Bull maintained their original full sugar variants in conjunction with existing sugar free products. Lucozade and AG Barr chose to reformulate with reduced sugar versions of their key brands to avoid the levy.

Although AG Barr comprehensively tested the reduced sugar IRN-BRU recipe with consumers and had the new products' acceptability confirmed by the completely independent *BBC One Show*, many consumers in Scotland were not happy. Campaigns to 'bring back IRN- BRU' were launched on Facebook and retailers who stockpiled the old full-sugar products ended up selling cans for up to eight pounds each! Despite the consumer backlash, AG Barr's board were reluctant to bring back full-sugar IRN-BRU. They introduced a full-sugar, high caffeine IRN- BRU Energy and then a Limited Edition 1901 style IRN-BRU after I had left but did not fully accede to consumers' wishes. However, in March 2021, they did announce that 1901 IRN-BRU would remain a permanent part of the range. Whilst this wasn't exactly what consumers wanted it was a gesture to meet part-way. It is possible for a brand to do a 'U-turn' with consumers and become even stronger, which you will read about later.

Having spent so long working in FMCG, the concept of brand loyalty has always been salient with various tools and measures used to track and monitor it. In Breaking Big by The Business Doctors, they make an interesting point; "If you really believe that customers will stay loyal to your brand simply out of habit or comfort or personal loyalties, it's time to think again".

Over the years I have witnessed the growth, but also the demise of many brands. In some cases, I have been convinced that decline was due to excessive meddling by marketeers and brand managers wanting to leave their mark on a brand through new positioning, packaging changes or reformulation. Of course, we all accept that you cannot stand still in business however, individual ego or ambition should never come before what is right for consumers.

When I started my career, New Product Launches were quite few and far between though the pace of development and launches of new products increased exponentially. The failure rate tends to be high and FMCG companies profit & loss accounts often carry quite significant amounts for write off costs. With the examples of Energy Shots and Squash'd, at least AG Barr avoided two of them!

Michael Porter of the Harvard Business School reflects both the Procter & Gamble and Lord Price approach when he said that "Strategy is about making choices, trade-offs; it's about deliberately choosing to be different".

I have never made claim to great strategic insight and am content to describe strategy loosely as the processes, plans and choices to bring about a desired future, such as achievement of a goal or solution to a problem, which requires effective planning and efficient marshalling of resources. Something like that anyway!

Or more succinctly, as I say to SMEs now, strategy is about making the right choices for growth. Tactics are the means by which a strategy is carried out, through planned and improvised activities to deal with current demands and deliver objectives supporting the longer-term goal. If anyone feels the need to improve on these definitions, I am certainly happy to be educated!

Finally, I have often considered the idea of a specific strategy document as something like a grail quest. Yes, sometimes a grand strategy or plan is succinctly captured and shared around an organisation for all to consider, like a written constitution. However, often a strategy evolves and develops less formally, more like the UK's unwritten constitution than a sacred strategy scroll to be held and cherished.

Budgets and Targets

There is one other important point to make, about monitoring and measuring progress - an old adage that I've found invariably holds true. 'You get what you measure' or 'what gets measured gets done'.

There is a caveat though. This only works if the goals, targets and objectives are sensible, or SMART:

- Specific
- Measurable
- Achievable
- Relevant
- Timebound

When I started with Procter & Gamble, the acronym was SMAC which stood for Specific, Measurable, Achievable and Compatible. The SMART version came later though the R was for Realistic. It has been suggested that Achievable and Realistic are effectively duplicates and proposed that the R should be for Relevance. This was a great intervention as you will see in the next chapter.

Two examples highlight the importance of getting budgets and targets right, or SMART, specifically the A part.

The year 2018 was the hottest summer in the UK for over forty years, which of course was good news for the sales of soft drinks and ice cream. However, in July 2019, AG Barr issued their first ever profit warning and in the annual report for results ending in January 2020 the chairman wrote, "Looking back, we did not fully recognise the extent to which we benefited from the hot summer of 2018. The budget set for 2019 was too optimistic versus the exceptional weather in the base." Their 2019 budget was overly ambitious and unachievable. It was SMRT. As sales director I did suggest this at the time…

During a short stint working at Flavour Warehouse one of my first tasks was to develop a sales budget for the next financial year, starting from December 2019. The new chief financial officer was not due to start for a couple of months and being inexperienced in the vaping category I consulted previous years' budgets and sought the input of the owner, head of sales and members of the finance team. The budget was approved, but I started to question the robustness of the assumptions. Certain parts of the business were not performing as well as initially suggested and the growth expectations made me uncomfortable. Vaping then became the centre of a negative media storm in the US, which had an impact on category performance. One month into the financial year I asked the question in a board meeting as to whether we should consider revising the budget expectations so that we would not spend a year of frustration and demotivation chasing numbers that were only *SMRT*. Unfortunately, there was no support for this idea.

I completely understand that it is not good practice to continually adjust a business' numbers, particularly in a listed company. Also, 'soft' or reduced targets are not the recipe for aggressive and consistent growth. However, when budgets or targets are not SMART from the outset you are also unlikely to get the performance that you aspire to.

I have always been as driven to hit my targets as any salesperson, due to professional pride and not just because they were linked to bonuses and remuneration, but without budgets and targets that are SMART, despondency can spread through the organisation.

Again, there can be an element of greyness in this area. You get what you measure is a great principle but depends on the accuracy of the measuring and having properly calibrated (SMART) benchmarks.

POINTS TO PONDER

- Strategy and Leadership are frequently used words in business, but not everyone understands them.
- Meeting a competitor's strategy head on can often be appropriate so long as it isn't 'monkey see, monkey do'- how can you differentiate?
- It takes courage and conviction to do the opposite of your competitors and there are no guarantees of success.
- Listen to consumers and do not be afraid to admit to a mistake.
- If Objectives or Goals are not SMART, people can (and will) switch off.

CHAPTER 11 - R & R

I found this interesting quote from Kevin Roberts, CEO of Saatchi and Saatchi.

"Here is my equation for success on brands and business:
[IQ+EQ+TQ+BQ]CQ"

(Translation: Intelligence, emotion, technology, bloody quick, with a creativity quotient.)

I really like Kevin's idea, though my success formula is a little simpler:

$$R + R = \nearrow$$

From my earliest days in Procter & Gamble I realised that successful outcomes were largely driven by the power of your brand and how productive your relationships were with your customers (that is retailers, wholesalers). Your relationships would allow you to get a product onto the shelf, whilst product relevance would ensure shoppers would take it off the shelf and purchase.

Over time I refined my thinking to conclude that Growth (or success on brands and business as in Kevin Roberts description) was essentially down to R&R.

R&R can mean many things depending on the situation, though the first one that springs to mind for me (as per collinsdictionary.com) is in the military context of rest and recuperation. Alternatives include a medical R&R (rescue and resuscitation) and a leisure focused R&R (relax and recreation).

From my experience in business R&R is the relevance of your proposition (to customers and consumers) and the relationship you have with them.

Therefore, as depicted below,

Relevance + Relationship = Growth

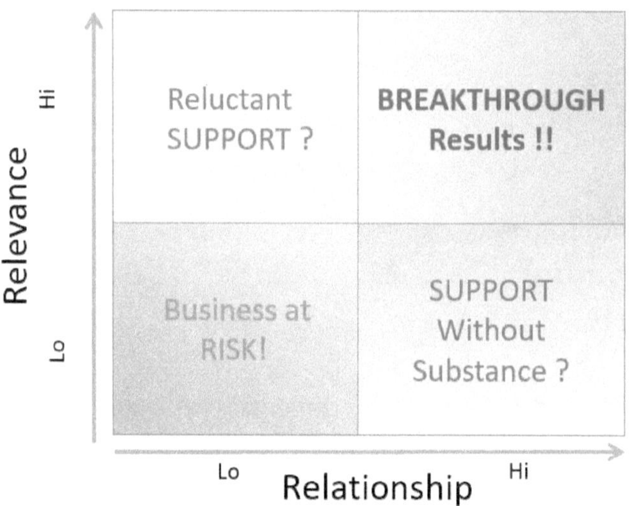

Business at RISK: If you have a weak product or service proposition then you tend to be of low relevance to your customers and if your relationships are poor and unproductive then your business, if you have any, will always be at risk and very unlikely to grow.

Reluctant SUPPORT: When relevance is high due to powerful branding, consumer understanding and high-profile marketing, or if you maybe have more niche products with strong loyalty and delivering decent customer profit, even if relationships are not that great your proposal is likely to be supported, even if reluctantly. Strong market leading companies (for example Procter and Gamble and Kellogg's) often tend to be in this box.

Retail and wholesale customers may view the supplier as too controlling or even arrogant however, they are so good at what they do that shoppers in their stores will demand the products. Not supporting them can put wider sales at risk. This was something we always leveraged on Pampers – it was the market leading nappy and the young families purchasing them were typically the highest spending shoppers. (NB: Our buying contacts sometimes referred disparagingly to Procter & Gamble people as 'Proctoids', suggesting that they were all similar men in grey suits, brainwashed with process and an absence of personality!)

One of the most sobering incidents and biggest learnings of my career came in a situation when I assumed a stronger relationship existed, than I actually had. Even though the relevance of Barr's proposition to the customer was high, my mistake put the relationship and business with a customer on the line. Fifteen years on, I still replay the incident and run through how I could have avoided it. The customer was a large discount chain, that the commercial director had managed personally through a direct relationship with the owner. I had been in the meeting where we had all agreed the plan, but a few months in we had provided the agreed investment, but the customer had only ordered a tiny fraction of the sales agreed. The CEO was worried and with my boss on holiday, having met the owner previously, I picked up the phone.....

After a friendly and cordial introduction, we 'danced' around a business update but eventually I had to raise the current situation of sales being way behind the agreement. After a few non-committal assurances, I flippantly suggested that we "weren't a charity" and needed to see a return on our investment. It was intended as a joke, but it certainly wasn't received that way! A torrent of expletives and threats to close the account boomed down the phone and I admit to being quite shaken by the reaction. I backpedalled furiously, apologised profusely and eventually the situation calmed down. I often referred to it with my team as an example of over playing a relationship and the story became something of a standing joke. The word *charity* was often used to put me in my place thereafter! Lesson learned big time – the meaning of the communication is the response you get.

SUPPORT without Substance: Sometimes individuals or even the whole company thrive on having great relationships with their customers even if their product or proposition is weak or not relevant. Sometimes this may be due to a historical relationship between company founders, or it may be that the supplier has over invested in key personal relationships. Or it could just be that certain individuals at a certain point in time really get on and like each other, so they do good business together. However, if the emphasis is based too much on relationship it may not endure changes in personnel so the support may lack substance over time.

In the early 80's Clive Sinclair had been the key driver of Margaret Thatcher's vision of a computer in every home ensuring Britain led the way in pioneering computer penetration. Through the ZX80, ZX81 and crucially the ZX Spectrum Sinclair enabled Britain to have the highest household penetration of personal computers in the world and made Sinclair a household name. He had delivered an affordable, hugely relevant product and secured a strong relationship with games mad teenagers and parents who genuinely believed that the Spectrum would enhance their education!

Unfortunately, Clive Sinclair's other great intervention did not enjoy the same respect and became an object of ridicule. As the Spectrum was a pioneer of home computing, the Sinclair C5 was to pioneer a new era of greener, electric personal transportation. A concept way in advance of Elon Musk and Tesla. However, the C5 could only really be described as a failure that destroyed the reputation of Sir Clive.

Why?

Despite having built such an outstanding reputation and relationships as an inventor and computing pioneer, and whilst the concept of electric personal transportation was relevant in an era of rising oil prices, the actual proposition of the C5 was fundamentally flawed. A lightweight electric vehicle, powered by a washing machine motor that could travel neither far, nor fast and accommodated the driver in a low horizontal position that was extremely vulnerable and insecure on the open road. Production problems, battery problems and a comedic sight on the odd occasion they were seen in public resulted in a total disaster. Sinclair had good Relationships and a positive reputation, but his proposition for changing commuter travel lacked true relevance.

Now of course, we have electric assisted bicycles, scooters and of course Tesla have pioneered the fully electric car. By 2035, the Government wants an end to production of Internal Combustion Engine (ICE) vehicles and all forms of transport to be fully electric. The electric transportation *concept* of the C5 is now hugely relevant, with current propositions getting stronger and stronger. Even so, it takes new entrants to the field a lot of time and investment to develop relationships and reputation. Tesla didn't make a profit in 15 years.

BREAKTHROUGH RESULTS: What can be achieved when relevance and propositions are really strong and the relationships even stronger?

When I joined, around three quarters of AG Barr's revenue came from IRN-BRU and a similar proportion of sales came from Scotland, where 5 million Scots drink 150 million litres of IRN-BRU in a year. The rest of the UK was almost considered as an export market, with only a small amount of business in London and the south. The soft drinks market still retains considerable geographic differences in the products consumed and the joke at the time was that Barr's business mirrored Bonnie Prince Charlie's advance – it petered out at Derby!

Being based in London with a predominantly southern footprint for their depots, Bestway's business with AG Barr was quite small. Relationships were good, but relevance was low. That all changed dramatically following two significant acquisitions and a new partnership in the mid noughties. Bestway acquired the Batleys group whose cash and carry heartland was the north of England and Scotland. AG Barr then agreed to launch US Energy Drink brand

Rockstar in the UK. Rockstar sponsored the high-profile boxing bout between Ricky Hatton and Floyd Mayweather providing an opportunity to showcase the brand by taking key customers, including Sir Anwar Pervez the Bestway Chairman, to Las Vegas to watch the fight. The following year, AG Barr bought the exotic juice brand Rubicon, the drink of choice for British Asian consumers and aside from Coca Cola, the key soft drink sold through Bestway's cash and carry estate.

The mutual business soon became much more relevant for both parties as AG Barr had the key soft drink in Scotland with IRN BRU (Scotland's 'other national drink') and in the London and south east markets with Rubicon. Bestway now had cash carries all across Great Britain. This was the start of a great business relationship which developed Bestway into AG Barrs biggest customer, even ahead of Tesco, and AG Barr became the second biggest soft drinks supplier to Bestway, behind only Coca Cola.

A strong 'Top to Top' relationship where the CEOs would join the sales and buying teams to align annual business plans filtered down to even stronger relationships within individual Bestway and Batley's cash and carry depots. Barr's commercial director had a love of cricket matched by many within the Bestway team, so as the Rubicon brand started to get involved with cricket sponsorship there became a mutual passion added to the mix. I was never good enough to participate personally however, an annual Bestway versus Barr Cricket match became a hotly contested event.

A unique business incentive programme was then agreed where the top performing branches would be rewarded by Barr hosting a trip to see the Cricket World Cup in Barbados. This was incredibly successful in terms of mutual sales and became a regular feature, eagerly anticipated by the Bestway team. The trip included an educational element to study local developments in soft drinks and naturally, had to be captured on AG Barr's Corporate Risk, Hospitality and Bribery Register. Other suppliers tried to run similar activities with their customers but what set the Bestway/Barr version apart was the genuine camaraderie. Whilst free time was available, we typically ate together and attended activities and sight-seeing as a full group with genuine friendships developing. In fact, one of the senior executives in Bestway commented that on many employees' desks, next to photos of their families, pride of place went to photographs from AG Barr trips!

Travelling to one of the events in 2016, I was sat in Business Class (only my second time ever – the first was a lucky upgrade!) on a BA flight to Las Vegas, with the then Managing Director, Martin Race. Martin is a highly respected, straight talking and down to earth leader, who earned great respect over a long career in wholesale. He has become a great friend and mentor and is always transparent and trustworthy. I related to Martin that my first experience of Bestway/Batleys was the grumpy old buyer in Liverpool and I never imagined that one day I'd be sharing a beer with the MD on route to the fun capital of the world !

AG Barr were awarded Bestway Supplier of the Year Award (as voted for by Bestway personnel) six times, at one point winning three years consecutively. The business grew exponentially and illustrates the breakthrough that is possible when you have a **highly relevant** proposition, combined with an exceedingly **strong relationship**.

POINTS TO PONDER

- Be sure of your relationship before you relax.

- When it comes to the crunch, Relevance trumps Relationship.

$$R + R = \nearrow$$

CHAPTER 12 – SOOTY SAYS NO!

The lion's share of my career has been selling and negotiating with customers, or more specifically spending hours of analysis, thinking and preparation for meeting with them. Old adages and acronyms like the seven P's (Proper Preparation and Planning Prevents Piss Poor Presentation) and PSF (Persuasive Selling Format) spring to mind. There are a plethora of training companies and consultants (many with similar FMCG backgrounds to myself) who have become specialists in the field and I've worked with many of them over time. Most claim that their approach is the definitive and most successful, but reality tells me that results usually come from a hybrid of their teaching and your own experience.

As a manager and team leader there are times when you simply have to 'be there' for your people. No matter how confident or experienced someone is, in business there is always the possibility of facing a completely new and challenging situation. Support and togetherness are crucial at times and a sales career in particular, can deliver great rushes of satisfaction but also exposure to confidence crushing and at times humiliating outcomes.

In *Netflix's* The Pharmacist, Chris Davis the former Purdue Pharma sales rep describes how as the negative PR around Oxycontin started to build, doctors would take his presentation or sales aid and just drop it straight into the bin. People face difficult scenarios in business and in all walks of life generally, but salespeople often face blunt rejection. They sometimes need supporting, picking up and reassuring as well as being given tools to help them learn from their difficult experiences.

Before Aldi and Lidl came to UK shores, the flag bearer for Discount Grocery in the UK had been Kwik Save, which was established in North Wales in the late sixties. Kwik Save prospered by selling basic brands, straight from their cardboard boxes, in no-frills stores with narrow aisles and wooden shelves: a quite unique, low cost, limited line operating model with huge success in Wales, the north of England and ultimately nationally. It floated on the Stock Exchange in 1970 and by the mid-1990s had more than a thousand outlets

When I managed Kwik Save for Procter & Gamble in the early nineties they were challenging and aggressive to do business with, but it was a great time to work with them. They continued to grow sales and market share and could also be great fun. In face-to-face meetings one of the buyers had a habit of breaking off from my presentation to suddenly dial up another supplier on speaker phone, making various demands, threats to de-list products and essentially bullying them. Hesitant at first, I used to sit there, twiddle my thumbs, and wait for him to turn back to me. Eventually, I told my manager what was happening and that I was struggling to deliver my presentations and hold the guy's attention. Of course, my boss realised he was just trying to unsettle me and suggested I needed to fight fire with fire. After that I would go to the call with a newspaper or a novel in my briefcase. When he started making calls I would sit back and read. After a while I was able to maintain his focus on what I was presenting.

You can view the buyer's behaviour as downright rude or just part of the game. If the latter, then he had learned from the master. The myths about some of Kwik Save's Trading Director's early tactics were legendary!

Major suppliers could not have envisaged, that Kwik Save would eventually become a FTSE 100 Company with a c.7% share of UK Groceries. Initially, relatively junior sales managers would be sent to Prestatyn to manage this small, idiosyncratic customer. The buying team became frustrated that the people they dealt with did not have the experience and authority to negotiate directly and make decisions face to face. Whether the following stories ever happened I do not know but given my experiences it seems likely that there would certainly be 'no smoke without fire' even if there has been a degree of embellishment over the years.

In one story, when faced with a sales representative who could not, or would not, make a decision on promotional investment or perhaps a request for improved pricing, the buying director would slide open a drawer in his desk, and remove a large pair of scissors. He would then lean across the desk, grab the Salesman's tie (all FMCG business was conducted in suits, shirts and ties in those days – in fact some companies insisted on bowler hats or trilbies until the sixties!) and cut it off halfway down. The person would then be told to leave the premises and advise their superiors to send someone with the authority to negotiate next time!

On another occasion, a Salesman from a drinks company was presenting a new product and encouraged the buying director to try the product as part of the sales pitch. The director said he did not need to try it himself to know whether it could be a sales success however, the seller was insistent. "Okay, I'll drink your product if you have a drink from me" the buyer conceded. After trying the new product, he produced a bottle of whisky from his drawer, filled a large tumbler and insisted the salesperson honour their pledge. He was then told that that three measures would take at least six hours to wear off and if seen driving his car beforehand would be reported to the police!

Probably the funniest and perhaps most humiliating of all the Kwik Save stories is when the eager salesman turns up, starts presenting and is suddenly told to stop. "Why do you keep looking at me when you should be presenting to Sooty?" the salesman is asked, as a Sooty glove puppet pops up from behind the desk and waves. "Sooty is doing the buying today" the buyer said and proceeded to insist that the rest of the presentation be directed at Sooty. At the end, Sooty whispers in the buyer's ear, he turns to the salesman and says, "Sooty says we are not going to stock your product".

If any of the above scenarios truly happened, how low would the salesperson have felt? Maybe, just maybe, the most experienced and thick skinned could have laughed it off, but how do you explain it all to your boss and how would they deal with it? I once used a similar technique in a role play with a younger, less experienced, but uber-confident member of the sales team. They were nearly in tears and that was only at an internal meeting! A few colleagues told me I was wrong to do it and maybe they were right, but better to take someone down a peg or two in a safe environment than leave it to a real-life situation.

Whether Sooty ever did say no, whilst I was with AG Barr, we faced a really challenging situation with a customer, which at the time gained quite a lot of publicity and contributed to the eventual introduction of GSCOP (The Grocery Adjudicators Code of Practice).As you shall see in the next chapter, I had to draw on the ancient art/science of alchemy to get the right results.

POINTS TO PONDER

- No doesn't always mean *no* – you just haven't made the proposition attractive enough to obtain a yes!
- Find a way to handle rejections and learn from disappointment. Do not just accept it.
- Aggressive behaviour in business is rarely personal, it is usually a tactic.

CHAPTER 13 - ALCHEMY

A university and Procter & Gamble colleague Jonathan Brown published a book in 2013 called *Stress and Success – Fast Fixes for Turbulent Times*. Having shared the manuscript upfront, Jonathan asked if I would add a testimonial at the start. In doing so I referred to ancient alchemy and the quest to transform lead into gold, comparing it to Jonathan's aim of turning stress into an advantage. Looking back at my career, I can see alchemy as a very appropriate metaphor when difficult and dire situations have been worked into successful outcomes

Soap Wars Part One

Procter & Gamble and Unilever were often considered to have created a duopoly in many home cleaning categories like laundry and dish care. It was not a true duopoly as there were of course several other suppliers to the market (though retailers own labels had not really taken off at this time). In the early nineties, Unilever fired a massive broadside at Procter & Gamble when they launched Persil washing up liquid to rival Procter & Gamble's Fairy Liquid, which was market leader by some distance. Persil was heavily backed with promotions, special offers and a heavyweight TV Campaign featuring comedian Robbie Coltrane (pre his role as Hagrid in *Harry Potter*). They secured good levels of distribution in the grocery multiples who were always keen to back a credible challenger to a market leader to lessen their strength and influence.

Procter & Gamble had to act fast and decisively, to defend Fairy Liquid. Persil was a challenger like non before and a massive investment in a UK defence plan was agreed. Procter & Gamble had become aware of Unilever's plans before Persil was actually on sale and wanted to get consumers to buy extra Fairy and 'pantry load' during Persil's initial trial period. This was before most stores had scanning facilities or the ability to do multi-buys and buy one get one free (BOGOF) promotions. Therefore, Procter & Gamble committed to producing huge quantities of twin packs, with two bottles banded together for a special price. On the smaller 500ml size there was a modest 25% price reduction, but on the 1 Litre there was an unprecedented deal of two for the price of one! Two litres of Fairy Liquid would take most families out of the market for months.

Even though the retailers were keen to support Persil, they couldn't refuse the strength of this offer, so Procter & Gamble had to allocate stock on the basis of customers' previous sales of the packs. For most this was fine, but with Kwik Save there was a problem. Being the original limited line discounter with a maximum of 2,500 products in any store, Kwik Save only listed 500ml Fairy Liquid in original and lemon flavour (2 shelf keeping units) and hence were not given an allocation of the 1 Litre BOGOF pack. On hearing this news, the trading director was furious threatening all kinds of sanctions against Procter & Gamble's range as they simply couldn't be seen without the best value pack. This would be a disaster for them in the eyes of consumers who shopped in Kwik Save for the permanently low prices and best value around.

At one point the outlook was grim. Kwik Save stopped ordering Fairy Liquid and were warning of other consequences. Their stores attracted millions of shoppers a week, so it was an unacceptable situation for Procter & Gamble too. A creative solution was desperately required and my manager at the time (Mr Baked Alaska) provided it. Procter would transfer Kwik Save's 500ml twin pack allocation to other customers and produce a new one-off amount of 1 Litre BOGOF stock just for Kwik Save who would commit to listing Original and Lemon Fairy 1 Litre on-going. From having no Fairy liquid in Kwik Save and a shattered relationship, Procter & Gamble then ended up with four sku's and huge displays in-store. I looked on this as business alchemy transforming a grim, lead like situation into glittering, shining gold. A lesson I would never forget.

These were the principles I employed in 2008 when pre-GSCOP Tesco put huge pressure on their supplier base for better terms, increased investment and improved pricing. Tesco's approach through brief, timetabled, simultaneous sessions with suppliers caused outrage and upset at the time. I approached it differently and took the learnings from Kwik Save to look at turning a potentially very damaging situation into a way of building the business in the future.

Discounter House: Be Afraid, Be Very Afraid.

In autumn of 2008 Tesco sent a massive shudder through the supplier base. Competition in UK grocery had 'hotted up' and ultimately prompted headlines like "Tesco posts worst figures in 16 years" (The Observer). Rejuvenated competition from the likes of Asda and Sainsbury plus the growing strength of Aldi and Lidl triggered a Tesco initiative that had furious MDs and CEOs writing to The Grocer about Tesco's brutal tactics and articles appearing in the mainstream national press.

My sales controller had been invited to a meeting with Tesco and I expected a debrief later in the day. I was surprised when he called literally fifteen minutes after the scheduled appointment and was concerned as I detected a tremor in his voice. My immediate concern was a car crash or some incident on route to Tesco Head Office in Cheshunt, but he explained that he had already been in and had the meeting. On arrival at Tesco House the usual meeting location, he had been re-directed to a new meeting facility just down the road, called Discounter House.

Discounter House was a large building that had been kitted out like a prison waiting room (if TV depictions are accurate!) with sparse furnishings and a series of open cubicles for one-to-one discussions with suppliers. Posters and Point of Sale materials describing Tesco as Britain's Biggest Discounter adorned the walls and displays had been built of a series of price fighter brands in key categories that were unique to Tesco. All very unusual and somewhat austere.

On sitting down in a cubicle with a buyer, with a dozen or so other suppliers in separate cubicles, my sales controller was presented with a single sheet of paper. This contained a brief summary of AG Barr's sales performance in Tesco, a request for improved pricing, increased promotional investment and a list of products that would no longer be ordered if everything wasn't agreed to within a week.

My first job was to provide comfort and reassurance to the controller who was genuinely quite shaken as he had not managed the Tesco account for long and could see our business being decimated. Next, I had to think objectively and rationally about the situation as it was approaching the company's financial year end and could have a major impact on our overall results. Stephen Covey's rattlesnake analogy from the *Seven Habits* came to mind, so rather than be angry or indignant like many suppliers were, I tried to relax and think about how we could turn this damaging situation into something positive.

As a relatively small supplier to Tesco, with most of our strength in the north, we'd typically found it difficult to secure Tesco support for our brands other than IRN-BRU in Scotland (claimed to be one of only two markets where Coca Cola isn't the unequivocal number one in soft drinks). With other, larger suppliers likely to fight Tesco with tooth and nail, and given Tesco needed something from us, I persuaded our understandably concerned board that if we met some of their requests quickly, we could be in a unique position to not just save products from de-list but go on the 'front foot' and request more support for our wider portfolio.

We followed this strategy through a series of meetings and follow ups, where I always ensured that I was on hand to support the sales controller. On one occasion I thanked the Tesco team for setting up Discounter House and commended it as a great opportunity for suppliers – I am not sure whether they took me seriously or not! In December, *The Telegraph* ran an article about Discounter House with quotes from suppliers about "outrageous" and "amoral" demands and concerns that Tesco would drive suppliers out of business.

Discounter House in 2008 was a shock to the grocery system, but by keeping an open mind, evaluating it as an opportunity and working as a team, we truly turned a leaden situation into a golden outcome. Our sales revenue with Tesco nearly doubled over the next twelve months and continued to develop strong and consistent growth thereafter.

Surfers and Swimmers

Other customers had similar investment objectives to Tesco although pursued them in different ways. Morrisons called suppliers in for a series of presentations where they shared that they had two different views of suppliers. Some were classed as 'Swimmers' because they put the effort in, worked hard with Morrisons and shared in mutual growth. 'Surfers' on the other hand enjoyed being carried along by Morrisons' progress without investing money or energy of their own. The follow up discussions were naturally quite different depending on how you were viewed as a supplier and it is quite possible that another category may have been informally introduced: 'drowned'!

Perhaps the most impressive approach to this type of discussions from my perspective, were Booker Wholesale. Groups of suppliers would be invited to one of their Cash & Carry branches where after tea, coffee and snacks the CEO Charles Wilson (one of the most impressive and sincere people in the industry and another Procter & Gamble alumni) would deliver a business update highlighting Booker's consistent growth and performance. Smaller groups would then be led by Booker personnel onto the shop floor and walked around to a series of quick presentations on various product categories and Booker's business plans. Then it was back for a summary presentation and Q&A with Charles and the trading team. Afterwards, you were given a letter outlining Bookers (investment) 'ask' and the negotiations would begin. A much more refined and civilised approach than the bleakness of Discounter House!

Breaking Point

One day I received a call from Tesco that was straight to the point. I was told that Tesco had a performance gap that it was looking to suppliers to fix. The soft drinks category had a target and within soft drinks Barr were expected to provide a certain value of support. I dusted down my 'alchemy instruction book' and suggested to Tesco what we would expect to get in return. An agreement was eventually reached, though it was nothing like as beneficial as in 2008. In fact, we were in disputed for quite some time with Tesco as to whether they had delivered what they'd agreed to.

In 2014, Dave Lewis took up the reins as Tesco CEO and what followed catapulted Tesco to the front pages – A £263m accounting scandal in over-stated profits and a subsequent fraud case. Christine Tacon had been named as the UK's first Grocery Code Adjudicator (GCA) the year before which was described by Consumer and Competition Minister Jo Swanson as "An incredibly important position in the retail groceries sector making sure that large supermarkets treat their suppliers fairly and lawfully". This brought the GCA and the Grocery Suppliers Code of Practice (GSCOP) into a much higher profile. The grocery industry and the behaviour of both suppliers and retailers had to change.

For a while it was 'open house' on Tesco with the written media and even *BBC Panorama* investigating Tesco in 2015 and describing how they 'turned the screw' on their suppliers as they struggled to deliver sales growth. Personally, I have experienced some rude, discourteous, and even quite t insulting behaviours from Tesco personnel. In the Panorama programme my former Procter & Gamble colleague David Sables, now CEO of Sentinel Management Consulting was interviewed and said that "bullying was going on in highly pressurised environments with threats" and Tesco were "extremely aggressive".

This also needs putting into perspective though. I have worked with some incredibly talented and decent people at Tesco and we British do have a tendency to 'knock our own'. On an individual level and perhaps even as policy, they undoubtedly 'crossed the line' on a regular basis but Tesco are an incredible success story overall and one of the leaders in global retail. Jamie Oliver gained a lot of plaudits for his campaign against obesity and pushed hard for the UK Soft Drinks Sugar Levy to be introduced in 2018. However, the credit should go to the initiative and product ranging strategy of then Tesco Soft Drinks Buying Manager, David Beardmore. David removed so many calories from the nation's diet that he probably deserves an MBE!

Negotiation

There are many training providers and books on negotiation. Clearly, the more effective you are, the more you can deliver for your organisation or for yourself in a domestic situation. It is a fascinating subject and should be a core competency for most people in business. When it comes to the big, strategic negotiations it pays to think big and not be afraid! Consider the cocept of shifting paradigms and do not be constrained. A big request means an opportunity to reciprocate with an equally big expectation, before the process flows to an outcome.

On one training programme I attended, a lot of attention was given to 'opening extreme', with a big request that is highly unlikely to be agreed. To an extent this worked for us in Discounter House, but you have to be careful that you don't undermine your own credibility from the start. When elected JCR President at University, one of my roles was to negotiate with the Warden of the hall of residence over the time for last orders in the bar. It was a residents' licence like a hotel and in theory could have served 24 hours. At my first hall event after election I was keen to impress those who had voted for me, and those who hadn't! I approached the Warden about a bar extension. "What time are you thinking?" he asked. His reply to my 3am request was "don't be so absurd – 12 o'clock no later" and walked off.

In a reverse scenario I utilised this after a summons to see Sainsbury.

They had requested a level of investment from Kellogg's that was not only ridiculously extreme, but they were offering nothing at all in return. Even though it was not his style, the senior buyer started the meeting with very bullish demands that we agree to the investment "or else"….My response was to say "or what? Am I going to find a horse's head in my bed?" in a reference to *The Godfather* film. There were four people in the room, it went very quiet and then we all burst out laughing. The ice was broken and eventually we had a productive meeting.

On another occasion I became really frustrated during a one-way exchange with Tesco where my contact kept talking over me and would not let me even complete a full sentence. In comic desperation, I raised up my arms and boomed out that the "Great Tesco has Spoken" mimicking when Dorothy and her gang finally get to meet the Wizard of Oz. For a few moments I thought I had gone too far, but eventually the tone softened and the interaction did become more of a two-way discussion.

The Equalizer

When we had more limited TV choice in the 1980's, one programme I really enjoyed was *The Equalizer*. The series was later turned into a film with Denzel Washington. In the original, tough guy actor Edward Woodward played a retired intelligence agent with a mysterious past, who uses the skills from his former career to exact justice on behalf of innocent people who are trapped in dangerous circumstances. Woodward was Robert McCall (American mum, British dad) and oozed style with a high-end apartment, cruising around in a Jaguar XJ6 and sporting a classic trench-coat. Essentially, he was a vigilante in New York City turning the tide on various villains and organised crime.

To enlist The Equalizer's support, people responded to a newspaper advertisement (no Internet in those days of course).

'Got a problem? Odds against you? Call the Equalizer: 212 555 4200.'

During tough, tense negotiations with customers, I bet many who would have loved to have brought in Robert McCall to hand out some tough justice! In reality, that role has probably been assumed by various training companies and management consultants. You can now contact the likes of Dave Sables and Sentinel through their website rather a classified advert in a newspaper.

Soap Wars Part Two

Before moving on, another duel between Procter & Gamble and Unilever is worth a mention. In the constant quest for the perfect laundry product, they were continually looking to upstage each other with new formulations, new dosing regimens, liquids, powders, gels and compact products.

In 1994 Unilever launched Persil Power to gain the upper hand on Procter & Gambles' flagship laundry brand Ariel. It then all 'kicked off like never before' in somewhat comical fashion, though billions of pounds were at stake. Procter & Gamble bombarded journalists across Europe with colour photographs of tattered rags washed in Persil Power detergent next to pristine garments laundered with Ariel. Procter & Gamble also commissioned lab tests showing how Unilever's Power detergent damaged clothes. They didn't just confine attacks to public relations they also ran full page newspaper ads developed by Saatchi & Saatchi claiming that Persil Power 'rotted underpants' and condemning the brand. Even for those of us working in Procter & Gamble this was a bold and unprecedented step that took us all by surprise – and caused a few giggles too. Remember the phrase about not washing your dirty linen in public?

Unilever, which spent £100m over five years developing Persil Power, vehemently denied the accusation, taking out full-page newspaper advertisements to get its message across.

The *Independent* reported on the Soap Wars in June 1994 showing a pair of Marks & Spencer boxer shorts at the centre of the dispute which Procter & Gamble says it washed sixteen times using its own Ariel Ultra and an identical pair with the opposition's Persil Power - alleging that Persil Power reduced the undies to a tattered state.

In January 1995 Sainsbury and Waitrose, two of Britain's largest supermarket groups removed Persil Power from their shelves following a similar announcement by Tesco, which said it was phasing out the detergent and replacing it with Persil New Generation, a detergent soon due for launch by Lever. Eventually, in a relatively low-key presentation a Unilever Executive admitted the issues with Persil Power a few years later and the launch is remembered as one of the great marketing fiascos.

POINTS TO PONDER

- Humour does have a place in business – it is about judging where and when to use it.
- Be bold but not foolish in negotiation.
- Open extreme but not so extreme that you put credibility at risk.
- Utilise all resources available and never be afraid to call for help from an Equalizer.
- In tough situations, think of the ancient art of alchemy. How can you turn lead into gold?

CHAPTER 14 - SCALEXTRIC

I have always had a passion for keeping life simple, for example limiting my use of social media to a few key applications so I don't get confused! I view business in a similar way. Allan Leighton, former CEO of Asda and chairman of Co-operative was the first person I heard say that "simplicity is divinity" and I've never heard of a leader going into a business with a strategy to make it more complicated!

Certainly, the operations directors I worked with in FMCG would prefer a business model like a Scalextric Racing Set. You set up the track into a circuit and race the cars around as fast as you can. Occasionally they come off (all production lines need downtime and inevitably you get the odd breakdown) but essentially, it's a very simple concept. Whilst it is quite straightforward to apply this analogy to the operations and manufacturing within a business, it is a more cerebral concept that can impact individuals across the *whole* organisation.

The more categories, products, brands, and individual SKUs in a business, manufactured across multiple production sites, coupled with broad ranging consumer communication and marketing activities plus various levels of pricing and promotional strategies, products suspect to VAT or VAT exempt, plus other government rules and regulations on where products can be sold and to whom, starts to put real pressure on peoples' mental bandwidth (just like this long sentence !).

Over time businesses grow 'arms and legs' and branch out into different sectors and markets. Clearly, there are many cases of diversification being part of a robust and effective strategy. When markets mature and growth becomes difficult, businesses can continue to grow and evolve by launching into different product categories.

Various products in history have also been developed as by products from the manufacturing of other goods. Wright's Coal Tar Soap was developed by William Valentine Wright in 1860 from liquor carbonis detergens, the liquid by-product of the distillation of coal to make coke; the liquid was made into an antiseptic soap for the treatment of skin diseases.

Many companies have expanded from their product origins into linked or adjacent categories. Procter & Gamble started as candle makers and now operate in scores of household goods markets, from laundry products and nappies to cosmetics. Historically Procter & Gamble were also manufacturers of hot beverages and snacks. Kellogg's cornflakes were developed by Dr John Harvey Kellogg (an 'interesting' and somewhat controversial character that readers can Google) at his Battle Creek, Michigan Sanitorium as a medicinal product. His brother Will Keith was the business brain behind The Kellogg Company which now operates in various food and snacking categories today. They now own Pringles, which they bought from Procter & Gamble for $2.7B. Barr Soft Drinks started out as a cork cutter supplying stopper corks for glass bottles before moving into the manufacture of the soft drinks themselves.

Corporate branding such as Kellogg's, Nestle or Unilever provides trust and credibility to individual brands like Nescafe or Persil that fall into the next level of the branding hierarchy. Often companies decide to launch into other categories by 'bouncing' an existing, trusted brand name. For example, the Cadbury brands core business is chocolate confectionary, however the chocolate itself and Cadbury name is licenced to manufacturers in other categories such as drinks, cakes, ice cream, desserts. When Kraft bought Cadbury and formed Mondelez, they bounced the Cadbury name across to a variant of Kraft Philadelphia cream cheese. Whilst at Kellogg's the Special K brand had projects looking at cola and bread. Caterpillar is the US equivalent of JCB, specialising in heavy machinery, bulldozers etc also Cat branded footwear.

When such expansion is part of a well-researched and logical strategy then all is usually well and good and adds to an organisation's sales and profit. A multi-category business like Unilever may have the equivalent of twenty Scalextric tracks all running at once, the point is that they are still in operational and cerebral terms relatively straight forward to manage.

Sometimes though, there can appear little link or logic to the collection of enterprises. Tomkins Group used to be known as the 'buns to guns' group such was the diverse nature of businesses owned, from Hovis bread and Mr Kipling cakes to Smith & Wesson handguns!

For a variety of reasons some businesses in fact develop into more of a Hornby train set. In common with Scalextric, the trains have a central circuit, but the layout becomes more and more complicated as points, sidings, branch lines and level crossings are added. The passenger trains are required to stop at stations and have to be closely co-ordinated, so they don't crash into freight trains. The whole system is more complex and hence much slower and more susceptible to breakdown. In the diagram, the two car Scalextric layout is much simpler than the Hornby Train system.

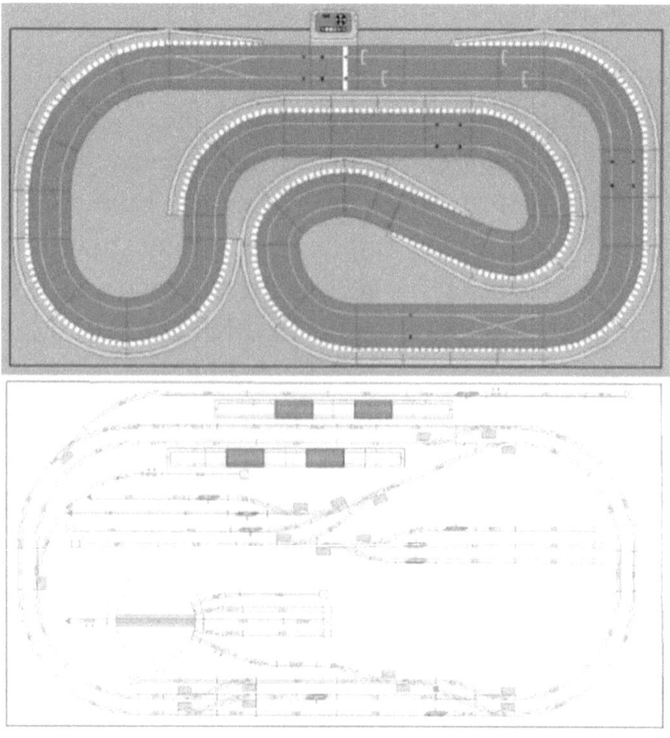

This point is reinforced in General Stanley McChrystal's *Team of Teams* showing how organisations can stray from being complicated to being complex, which results in blurred focus, inefficiency and ultimately reduced effectiveness.

Why does this happen?

There can be many causes. From my experience it is when a business is run more by 'personality' than 'process'. Procter & Gamble was a business with very strong and established processes. Individuals tweaked and evolved processes over time. Essentially people come and go, moving on to other roles and assignments, yet the core processes are robust and roll on. I've experienced other organisations that appeared to be driven more by the personality of key individuals, with the underlying processes being weak and subject to radical change. This can lead to more short-term and 'knee jerk' decision making, less underpinned by process and consistency. To me this has a variety of causes:

- Imbalance of control and influence, in a management group who cannot deal effectively with conflict.
- The inability to say "no" and *The Emperor's New Clothes* scenario where no one has the courage to point out the obvious.
- Unchecked enthusiasm in a business run more by personality than process.
- Immaturity in someone with authority who acts like the proverbial 'child in a sweet shop' reaching out for everything, because they can.
- An element of greed – 'we can have a piece of that' - without proper evaluation of the opportunity.
- Ignorance of the true costs (time, money, resources) and implications

Some of these elements combined can result in 'toxic positivity'. I have witnessed and been frustrated by this during my career. Whilst knee-jerk, ill-considered reactions to every problem, issue or challenge are neither required nor constructive (i.e. 'flapping' and panic), toxic positivity can prove just as damaging to an organisation as apathy.

I also encountered senior people insistent on holding off on confronting or communicating issues to an extent that it can border on dishonesty. They can demonstrate a steadfast refusal to accept the reality staring them in the face because of their overly optimistic belief that things may improve. Instead of a transparent, open approach when a problem arises, they keep covering it up, hoping it will get better. Eventually they have an even bigger, costlier mess to deal with.

I won't stray too far into areas where I don't really have the competence to add much value. Therefore, I would encourage readers to study David Snowden's Cynefin framework, which assesses the difference between complicated and complex systems.

Kellogg's Krispy Bisks – the launch that never was.

Some of the above points become manifest in the story of Kellogg's Krispy Bisks.

There were similarities between Kellogg's and Procter & Gamble. Historic blue chip American multi-nationals with strong positions in their respective categories. Whilst Procter & Gamble typically 'lock horns' with Unilever in detergents, Kellogg's arch-rival in breakfast cereal is Weetabix.

Kellogg's were the overall cereal category leaders through their flaked (Cornflakes, Frosties, Special K) and rice-based products (Rice Krispies, Coco Pops). Weetabix were number two overall but dominated in biscuit-based and hot cereals. Cereal Partners Worldwide (Nestle/ General Mills) were also consistently growing share and private label products were grabbing a greater piece of the action

A year or so before I joined, Kellogg's had appointed a blunt, straight-talking Australian as UK MD who had come in and really started to shake up the business. One of his key acts was to make a new sales director appointment, promoting a bright, driven and ambitious internal candidate, who clearly had an eye for talent and recruited yours truly! One of their objectives was to go 'on the front foot' against key competitors whilst simultaneously driving hard on Kellogg's core brands.

To take on Weetabix's dominance in breakfast biscuit cereals, Kellogg's marketing and innovation team set out to develop a top-class product to challenge them. Through consumer research they identified that Weetabix's weakness to certain consumers was that the products turned soft and mushy quite quickly when milk was poured over. Great for feeding infants and toddlers, but less desirable for many older consumers. A product was then developed that would retain its crispiness longer in milk and the brand name was agreed – Kellogg's Krispy Bisks.

This was a major, high-profile initiative for Kellogg UK and my responsibility was to lead the Sales input within the project team and plan the customer execution.

A significant amount of time and funding was invested as this was such a strategic play, including full use of BASES testing (a simulated test marketingtool suite). We were confident that we had a winner!

Artwork and branding were developed, and an advertising campaign was commissioned to emphasise the crispiness of the product in milk. Distribution targets with key customers were set and a full in-store promotion and point of sale material plan was developed. We then started to go and sell customers on this fantastic new launch for the cereal category and the results were really encouraging. Strong distribution agreements were secured with the key grocery multiples.

What could go wrong?

Not a lot really, we were on the edge of glory except for one relatively minor detail…manufacture of the product itself.

Kellogg's did not have the manufacturing capability to produce biscuit like products and searching Europe for a manufacturer who could produce enough product for launch did not prove fruitful. A year or so before, Kellogg had launched an extruded cereal called Crispix which was produced in the Far East and shipped across. An extruded cereal is one where several different grains are all mashed together, extruded into the required shape, and then baked. Typically, they were quite strong products which held their form well. In Crispix's case this was a lattice.

A similar arrangement was proposed for Krispy Bisks when a manufacturer with sufficient capacity was identified in Australia. I remember sitting in the project meeting when this was proposed and like my other colleagues, nodding and deferring to our supply chain colleagues' greater knowledge. A few comments were made in private afterwards, but no-one spoke up to challenge the wisdom of shipping across container loads of light, brittle wheat biscuits halfway around the world. The emperor may well have been naked, but we carried on with the launch plans.

Initial product samples for customers were air freighted over straight from the production line and all was good. We were on to a winner and the pipeline stocks were due to arrive a week or so before our go live day in-store.

Then came an early morning call from the Sales Director to attend an urgent project update meeting!

The first stock had arrived and when the container was opened and samples checked, the bisks had broken up and crumbled into a powder. Further quality control checks would be done, but we needed to be ready to advise customers.

Disaster!

Pretty much every box opened was the same, the launch would have to be cancelled ten days or so before it hit the customers' shelves. Promotions had been booked, Krispy Bisks had been included on new shelf layouts and the sales teams had to make embarrassed, red-faced phone calls to buyers and deal with the ensuing demands for compensation, costs of re-writing planograms and wasted point of sale materials.

If ever I experienced a case of the Emperor's New Clothes in my career, then this was it. With hindsight it was a crazy logistical plan to ship a delicate product across the seven seas, but no-one had the foresight or courage to question the plan.

False rumours later circulated that Weetabix had 'paid' Kellogg's to stop the launch, which saved Kellogg some face and in the highly unlikely event it was true, it was well above my pay grade.

Sometimes, unexpected external events can act to your advantage. Attention was quickly diverted away from Krispy Bisks as a UK fuel crisis commanded the highest priority focus for retailers and suppliers alike. Ensuring continuity of supply across the whole store enabled Krispy Bisks to slip into the shadows with embarrassment minimised. Interestingly though, despite this disater, the MD eventually took up the CEO position in the US.

From my perspective, I was determined to be very wary of Emperor's New Clothes syndrome going forward and decided that if ever I had fundamental concerns or even nagging doubts about a project, I would air them. This happened when I moved into a marketing role on children's cereals. The consistent rise of Cheerios was proving a thorn in Kellogg's side as they did not have an extruded multi-grain product which could compete. We set to work to produce a product under the Rice Krispies banner, as a contemporary offering from Snap, Crackle & Pop (the three elves who promote the brand). Instead of one shape, to increase kids' interaction with the food, we produced a series of shapes like trees, people, stars etc (similar to the old Heinz Noodle Doodle brand).

The product created seemed good enough, especially with the addition of pre-biotics to aid the digestive system (this why I spent a day discussing poo and wind as mentioned earlier) and Snap, Crackle & Pop were certainly up for it. The problem was deciding on a name. Various advertising and brand naming agencies were consulted over quite a length of time to get a perfect name. Cheerios has a nice, positive up-beat sound to it, so when the name finally proposed was presented, I just had to put my name up and object. To me 'Muddles' was too negative sounding. My daughter was four at the time and target audience for the product. As a parent I did not want my child getting in a muddle, it just wasn't a positive vibe. I offered 'Snapseez' as an alternative, the idea being that kids could match up the shapes. Not a great name either, though I considered it to have less negativity than Muddles. I was over-ruled, and it launched as Muddles. Not that long afterwards when I'd moved to AG Barr, I noticed in a store that the product name had changed to Kellogg's Rice Krispies Multi Grain Shapes – wow! What a slick name, it just rolls off a toddler's tongue!

POINTS TO PONDER

- Be a student of simplicity and not an arch overcomplicator
- Think of simple, Scalextric type solutions and avoid the complications of Hornby.
- If you spot something that others can't (or don't want to) see, ask if the emperor really is wearing new clothes?

CHAPTER 15 – SEEING THROUGH THE MIST

What can be done to aid prioritisation and help people see through the mist to understand what is most important?

As AG Barr's portfolio started to expand through NPD (New Product Development) and product acquisitions the sales team became confused as to which brands and initiatives were the most important and how much of their time and focus should go against different projects. We had lots going on. To help them, I went back to another old, but familiar model – Maslow's Hierarchy of Needs, where lower order needs must be met before you can move up to the next levels of the pyramid and compared this to our product portfolio.

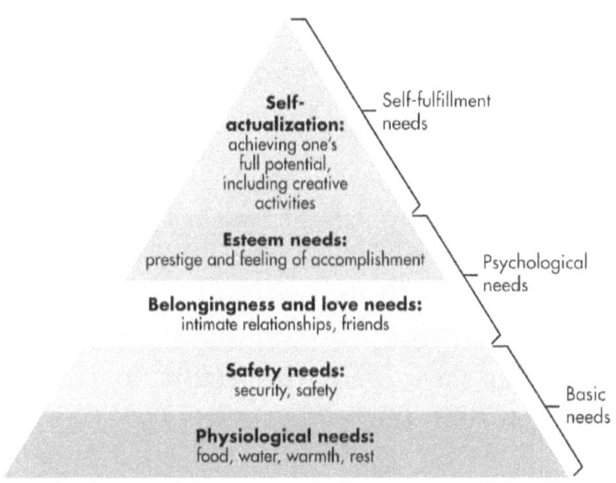

In most FMCG businesses there tend to be a few core brands or products that effectively underpin everything else. They contribute the most sales and profit but also generate production efficiencies and economies of scale supporting newer, smaller, or more specialised brands. Sometimes this can be captured by the 80/20 or Pareto concept, ie 20% of the product range produces 80% of the sales. Keeping these products in good health and performing well are the

'Basic Needs' of the organisation. Failure to manage them carefully in the here and now, will undermine attempts to grow the business by launching new products and ideas, which rely on the reinvestment of profit generated by the established brands.

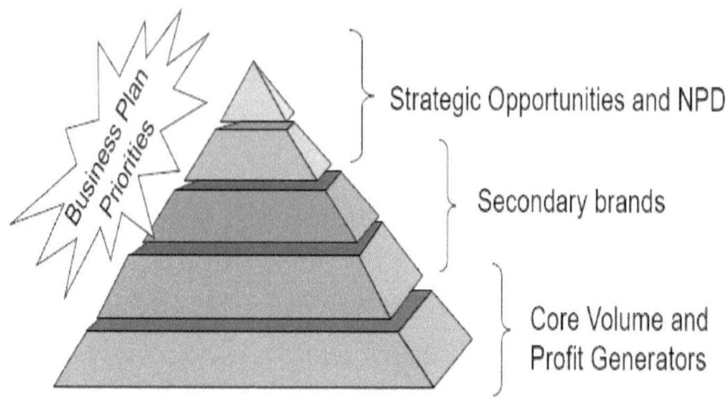

In AG Barr, the Basic Need brand - the core volume and profit generator by far was IRN-BRU. In fact, Barr had traditionally positioned itself as the IRN-BRU Company, though overtime we focused on becoming Barr Soft Drinks, representing a change in philosophy, not just name. At Kellogg's, standard Cornflakes were key. Not only were Cornflakes a category and grocery icon, but they were the base for two other crucial products. With added sugar they became Frosties and with the addition of nuts and honey they were Crunchy Nut Cornflakes. These products were priced higher. Reflecting this, Kellogg's manufacturing facility at Trafford Park was the biggest cereal factory in the world.

At Flavour Warehouse where I had a short assignment, even if you took out most of their e:liquid flavours, they would still have a very viable business from just two: Pinkman and Heisenberg.

Applying the Maslow analogy to the AG Barr product portfolio identified to the sales team which brands represented their 'bread and butter'. Of course, they were not permitted to ignore other products and were also measured on NPD results, but it ensured they had clear priorities.

The other common analogy with which most are familiar is of course the good old 'leaky bucket', where it is no good investing in NPD and initiatives to pour new business in at the top, if your base business dribbles away through holes in the bottom of the bucket

N.B. Maslow's Hierarchy of Needs is clearly showing its age. Had it been developed today it would probably be more like this:

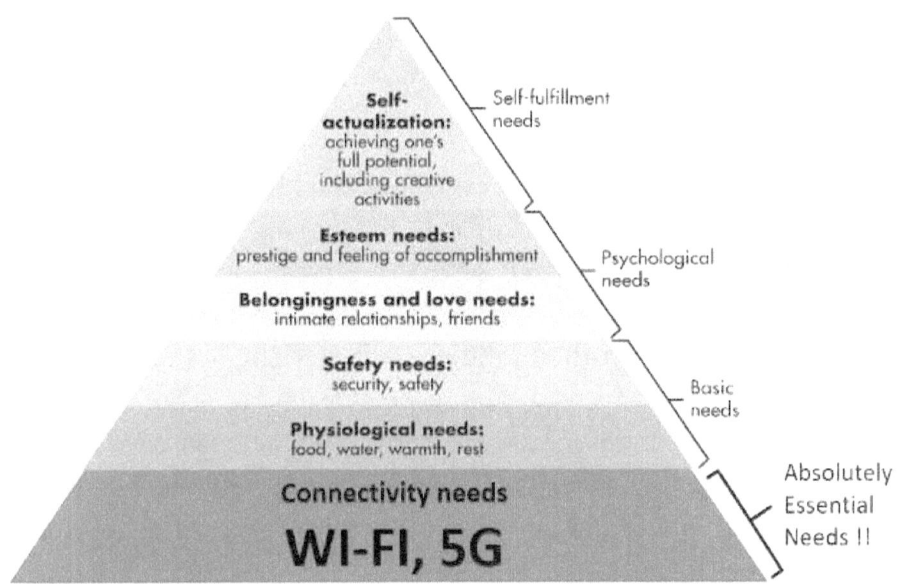

CHAPTER 16 – FUN AND GAMES

Promotion is one of the classical four Ps of marketing (along with product, price and place) taught at university. Promotion in its broadest sense refers to all activities designed to create awareness and encourage purchase of a brand, product or service. This includes TV advertising, print advertising, public relations and these days of course digital marketing is dominant through on-line presence and social media.

In FMCG it is the brand managers who typically have responsibility for all the activities run from the product packaging itself (competitions, mail-ins etc), within the packaging (for example a free toy in a cereal pack) or through media vehicles such as TV, websites, social media, radio and print. With the brand characters Kellogg's created such as Tony Tiger, Coco-Monkey, Snap, Crackle & Pop and Captain Ric (Ricicles) and the high-profile licencing agreements and sponsorships they secured such as Disney, Warner Brothers, Star Wars and British Athletics (to name but a few) there was always great fun to be had.

Similarly at AG Barr, IRN-BRU linked up with the Scottish and English Football Leagues and Super League Rugby. Rubicon became the official soft drink of the England and Wales cricket team , whilst Rockstar had some really exciting tie ups with boxing (Hatton v Mayweather, Froch v Groves), Mixed Martial Arts, game releases and various music festivals.

In an FMCG sales role, the promotions on which significant time and effort is spent on are the ones consumers see when they enter a store. These are executed by the retailers. Most instore promotional offers these days tend to be simple price reductions or multi-buy offers eg Buy 3 for £5.

Many graduates starting an FMCG career will have been given a promotional effectiveness project at some point. When I arrived at Kellogg's they had invested in a software package called Trade Promotion Management (TPM) to provide such analysis. However, it worked by analysing past promotions and the promotional landscape had suddenly changed dramatically with the emergence of Every Day Low Pricing (EDLP) and Safeway's extremely deep price cut promotions (pricing 'guerrilla' tactics called Gonzalez). All the sales controllers knew that TPM was of little use at that point, but as the newcomer I was given the 'hospital pass' and had to tell the European President that a project he had championed and provided significant investment for was already obsolete.

Occasionally you do see something quite different, but typically neither retailers or suppliers want the complication, nor have the patience to run more complicated activities. That wasn't always the case and I've been involved with various brands and customers where in conjunction with buying a certain product, the shopper would be rewarded by a free gift with purchase such as breakfast bowls, drinking glasses, storage vessels etc.

Persistence Pays

At Kellogg's there had been recurring discussions in business planning sessions about how it would be great to have a Kellogg branded free cereal bowl promotion in the key grocery stores, but it was considered a sort of 'holy grail' promotion that would never be achieved. It was a challenge I took on and eventually we did indeed run several such promotions which performed really well. Firstly, we utilised Kellogg's sponsorship of GB Athletics to execute a free Olympic Bowl in 2000. Only a couple of customers agreed to execute it due to the complexity however, it performed well as customers could take home a free high-quality ceramic bowl when they purchased two packs of Kellogg Cereal. We ran a similar promotion the following year, though just on Crunchy Nut Cornflakes, but with more customers participating the promotion gained momentum.

The FIFA Football World Cup in 2002 was taking place in Japan and South Korea. Unusually, this meant that matches in the UK would kick off in the morning due to the time difference. Large sporting events are crucial sales opportunities for brands and retailers, though in this case, apart from diehards, the opportunity for beers, wines and spirits was appreciably less. This was an opportunity for breakfast products, though until David Beckham fired in a late free kick against Greece, England's participation was in the balance. With Wembley being re-built, that game was played at Manchester United's ground, Old Trafford – just a few hundred yards from Kellogg's head office. Fate.

After three years of patience and persistence trying to convince all the major UK retailers to manage the complexity of a free bowl promotion, we had our chance. By this point I was leading Kellogg's Tesco and Sainsbury sales teams and through lots of hard work and negotiation we led the way. For every two packets of certain Kellogg's cereals, the consumer got a free ceramic breakfast bowl, designed on the outside like a traditional panel football with a green inside with football pitch markings. We had advertising support on TV and posters with1.2 million bowls ending up in UK homes. We also received a global Kellogg Award for the year's best promotion.

The crowning glory was planned to be TV coverage of a World Cup sportsman's dinner that we'd agreed to sponsor for Caravan, the grocery industry charity. The event was at Preston North End's football stadium and all the surviving members of England's 1966 World Cup team (excluding Sir Bobby Charlton) were due to attend. TV and press coverage were lined up by our PR team and Tony the Tiger was looking forward to meeting the world cup heroes.

Unfortunately, footballer Roy Keane then intervened! He had walked out of the Republic of Ireland training camp at the World Cup and all the press wanted to do was interview Jack Charlton, the former Ireland manager. My poor bowls! They missed out on their moment of glory, though I did enjoy the company of a footballing hero, the late Alan Ball, until the early hours of the morning.

The Man in the Hathaway Shirt.

There was a famous printed advertisement in the 1950's for Hathaway Shirts created by David Ogilivy. Many marketeers will be familiar with the iconic image of the distinguished man with an eyepatch promoting and ultimately transforming the sales of the Hathaway Shirt Company in Maine. The eye patch was never mentioned in the advert but used as a mysterious prop to generate curiosity.

The man in the Hathaway shirt

On one creative marketing course I attended, we studied this landmark piece of advertising, or rather, we studied a video of others analysing it. Of course, the main discussion was around the eye patch – what did it add? Was it distasteful and should it be removed? Whilst there was no real relevance to the eye patch and several in the group said it should be removed various compromises were assessed. The conclusion was that removing it diluted a very powerful advert into a relatively bland piece of copy which wouldn't stand out.

Flexibility can be a very important quality in business, but the man in the Hathaway Shirt proves that sometimes, compromise can be a dirty word and ultimately render an idea worthless. I hold up my hand to some compromises during my career, with possibly the most pointless one being a promotion I ran as an account manager working on Asda.

It was the run up to Christmas and both the Pampers (nappies) brand manager and the Always (sanitary towels) brand manager were insistent on having in-store promotions. "All the promotion slots and display space are booked up" I replied. "The only way you can get a promotion is if you make a stand alone display shipper and they have to be Christmas branded". The brand managers were adamant promotion was crucial, and I felt compelled to find a compromise. We sent flat packed cardboard Father Christmas display shippers incorporating the message 'Buy Pampers, get Always Half Price' to stores so that they could load them with stock and site them in the health and beauty aisle. The brand managers were pleased – in theory they had their promotions. In practice it was a desperate waste of time and money. If even a dozen shippers got to the shop floor I would have been surprised (most went straight to the bin) and there was a problem scanning the promotion in-store for the first few days. I learned that if you compromise too much you might as well not bother!

On another occasion at Procter & Gamble, a brand manager brought a "fantastic idea" to me called the 'Lenortainer'. At the time, fabric conditioners were in plastic bottles as they still are, but Procter & Gamble had also introduced cardboard re-fill packs to save plastic waste. The Lenortainer was a 'de-luxe' Lenor bottle to be sold for 99p and sited next to the re-fills. "It has to be empty" said the brand manager "as we can't fill this bottle on the production line". I was slightly taken aback. "So, you want me to go Tesco, Morrisons and Asda and ask them to sell bottles of fresh air?" Needless to say, the Lenortainer never happened!

A Salutary Lesson.

Many people at Kellogg's developed a fascination or even an obsession with Tony the Tiger and Frosties. Tony had been trying hard on Frosties' behalf for many years, but unfortunately sales weren't "grrreat", in fact whilst still one of the largest brands by volume in the portfolio, sales had been declining year after year. Every senior manager or marketeer seemed determined to be the person who fixed Frosties, so it became a bit of a political football. So much so, that the CEO in Battle Creek, Michigan even got involved with the production of UK TV advertising at one point, due to escalating viewpoints in the Kellogg's and J Walter Thompson hierarchies (JWT were the advertising agency and along with Kellogg's brand managers, marketing controllers, directors etc, JWT personnel also wanted to be recognised as the ones who fixed this iconic, much loved but troubled brand).

The TV copy at the time had introduced a new villain, the evil Dr Cheetah, as Tony's arch-rival who was determined to steal the Frosties secret formula. Dr Cheetah sported a menacing eye patch, though he did not wear a Hathaway Shirt! As entertaining as the 'Batman Esque' advert was, it wasn't having a tangible positive effect, so in the brand planning sessions we decided that a more dramatic intervention was required.

A couple of years previously, before I had joined, a move towards brand efficiencies had seen the Coco Pops brand re-named Choco Krispies, consistent with continental Europe. However, there were quite a few disgruntled customers at the time (an era in which P&G changed Oil of Ulay to Oil of Olay and Jif became Cif for similar reasons). The Coco Pops advertising agency Leo Burnett hit on a radical idea which was one of the first truly interactive campaigns: The Coco Vote. Kellogg's decided to let UK consumers decide on the brand name. TV adverts were run with campaigners championing the names Coco-Pops and Choco Krispies and consumers were encouraged to vote via a freephone number or online (though it was still early days for the internet)

The result? An absolute landslide victory for Coco-Pops. TV copy celebrated the result, the packaging was changed back and Leo Burnett's in my mind had pulled off a game changing piece of advertising.

Returning to Frosties, as a sales and marketing team we discussed various ideas to re-invigorate Tony and the brand. One of the more radical questions asked was "has Tony had his day?". Was the aging tiger too long in the tooth and no longer relevant as we started the twenty first century? To remove Tony from the packaging and change the advertising strategy would be a major departure and even though his appeal may have faded with consumers he was a very much-loved feline within the Kellogg company.

Thinking back to the Coco Vote, I pondered if we could engage consumers once more and see if we could ride a wave of affection for Tony if we 'threatened' to dispense with his services. We then developed a cunning plan that Dr Cheetah would kidnap Tony and hold him to ransom. The public would have to pay a million 'lid' ransom to get him back.

Tony's image on the Frosties box would be removed and left as a blank shadow, whilst a pre-paid postcard would be printed on the box which kids could send in to help free Tony (with an on-line execution too, as this was now 2001!). We would provide TV updates and when a million lids/postcards had been received (or less if we considered it appropriate – this was a marketing plan, not a general election!) we would celebrate the release of Tony, he would regain the affection of the public and reclaim pride of place on the packaging. We all, myself especially, thought this would be a magnificent, highly visible campaign that would restore Tony and Frosties' pre-eminence in kids' cereal……

But.

After all our hard working and enthusiasm, the UK Board refused to sign off the campaign. I was absolutely gutted. Like everyone else, I wanted to be the person who fixed Frosties. I sought that honour and recognition, yet a brilliant plan was turned down. My initial anger subsided to feelings of disappointment, as the board explained that if there was an incident of a high-profile kidnapping or similar unfortunate event whilst the campaign was running, it would be in appalling bad taste to society, hugely detrimental to the brand image and cost a fortune if we had to remove product from stores in a damage limitation exercise. I was frustrated but over-ruled.

Several months later, after we had cobbled together an alternative though much weaker Frosties campaign, on a sunny afternoon in Kellogg's Manchester HO, a colleague popped into my office and said "Have you heard the news? Someone has flown a plane into the Twin Towers in New York". Everyone gathered around a small TV set and watched the awful footage. On September 11th 2001, four airliners had been hijacked, effectively kidnapping hundreds of people in the worst terrorist atrocity in history. A moment that those who witnessed it can never forget.

Had the Frosties Million Lid Ransom campaign been running at the time this would have been hugely distasteful and highly damaging for Kellogg's corporate reputation. The board had been right to block the Frosties' campaign. I was wrong and learned several lessons that day. Most notably, that no matter how good a business idea you think you have, you need to retain a degree of objectivity and be open to the counsel of others. Persistence and tenacity can be important qualities in business, but a sense of perspective is also vital.

As an aside, when I joined AG Barr in 2004, they had just launched a new TV campaign on IRN-BRU. The advertising idea was that the taste of IRN-BRU was so 'phenomenal' that the person drinking it would be so engrossed that they would be oblivious to unbelievable and incredible events unfolding around them. One of the TV adverts showed a tramp swept up and processed through a street sweeper vehicle and emerging well dressed and all 'spic and span'. Glasgow is IRN-BRU's heartland and ten years later a tragedy occurred on 22 December 2014 when a bin lorry collided with pedestrians in the city centre, killing six and injuring fifteen others. Timing can be crucial and clearly that advert is unlikely to ever be shown again.

A Snap & Crackle of an idea, that went Pop!

When I moved into a marketing role managing a portfolio of Kellogg's kids brands, my daughter was just a toddler herself. Like most children, she loved having stories read to her at bedtime, but such was her appetite that we often let someone else do the narration through story-time compact discs (CDs).

We had a gap in the On-pack promotional plan for Rice Krispies and needed a brand building idea that could develop the character of the elves Snap, Crackle and Pop and drive sales. Inspired by my daughter I developed an idea of a series of story CD's that would be free in the-pack.

Snap, Crackle & Pop had distinct personalities with Snap being the eldest, cleverest and most serious, Crackle the strong, silent type who provided the muscle, and Pop being the youngest, daft elf who was invariably a source of amusement to the others. Snap, Crackle & Pop would host the CD, like an elven Ant and Dec. As well as their banter and songs, each CD would feature several familiar fairy stories. As most fairy stories contain an important message, Snap would help the other two (and the listening children) to understand the moral of the tale. For example, the *Ugly Duckling* would encourage children not to judge others by how they looked and *The Boy Who Cried Wolf* would reinforce the danger of telling lies.

We commissioned an agency to work up scripts and songs for three different CDs and though it was a costly promotion I was convinced we were onto a winner. I had a vision of millions of kids bonding with Snap, Crackle and Pop learning important lessons on car journeys or tucked up in bed at night.

Whilst the Million Lid Ransom understandably and rightly, never came to fruition, it is one of my key regrets that the Rice Krispies story-time CD's never reached the public. Kellogg's had suddenly secured a new high-profile licence which took precedence to feature on all the key brands at the time the CDs were planned. Several years later I noticed McDonalds giving Story CDs as the gift with a Happy Meal and sighed as I knew that Snap, Crackle and Pop would have done a far better job!

POINTS TO PONDER

- Persistence and resilience are often key when you are trying to do something different.
- However, if an idea becomes diluted and compromised you may be best advised to drop it and move on to something else.
- Don't allow yourself to become too involved or attached to a project. Retaining an element of objectivity is key.
- Decisions in business are rarely personal.

A SENSE OF PERSPECTIVE

On one of the training courses when I started with Procter & Gamble, recognising that we were all young, determined, career focused individuals one of the senior managers wanted to provide a sense of perspective. He suggested that "of course business and your job are really important" but with oblique reference to Maslow he also commented on the need for "a sense of perspective – after all, you're only selling Soap Powder and there are people in this country living on the streets in cardboard boxes". I rather frivolously responded "Yes, but the more we sell, the more boxes they have to sleep in!". The comment achieved a round of laughter and got me onto the manager's radar but was not the most sensitive comment I've ever made.

Thirty or so years later, with maturity and greater humility I observed the changes in society brought on by the Covid-19 crisis, the subsequent lockdown and social distancing measures which certainly caused most people to think differently about our key workers and the role they perform in society. Nurses, medical staff and carers were at the forefront of efforts to keep us safe, with the police, military and various other public sector employers keeping the country running while the rest of us grumbled about the restrictions and worried about whether we would be able to go back to our jobs and careers.

The public out pouring of support, particularly for the NHS, helped to uplift the nation but the key concern is whether the 'NHS Heroes' will still be remembered as prominently in the future. It has been recognised by many that nurses in particular, are not financially rewarded sufficiently for the care they provide and most public sector workers do not earn as much as counterparts in private sector careers. And there are so many other key workers who should be rewarded.

I was humbled by the story below on LinkedIn and compelled to comment, 'We are all in debt to the NHS. 'Hats off' to their courage and commitment. Very humbling for those of us spending careers in business, just chasing the £££s.'

Short story from a young NHS Nurse.

This is how I left work this morning, after sobbing during staff handover. I feel it reflects the sad reality of how NHS staff are feeling every day at the moment.

Tonight, on my shift I had to tell the family of a dying man, that they cannot go in to see him, they cannot say goodbye to their dad and that they have to go home.

Think about that for a minute, how it must feel to tell a family that.

This is after finding out one of my patients had died yesterday after testing positive for the corona virus. I know this is happening all over but the patient group I look after, I really feel they don't deserve this. Battling cancer with every fibre of their being, having chemo, radiotherapy and everything that comes with that and then to die alone, unable to have visitors, say goodbye to their loved ones. Wards unable to support their family the way we want to because family can't visit. How can this be happening, how is this fair? How on earth will families get closure? Can you imagine your parent dying along and not being allowed to see them?

Don't the public want to do their bit to stop this from happening? Why is it so hard to just stay inside? And the truth is I'm filled with dread, because I know this is going to get worse.'

Similarly, shop workers kept us supplied with key provisions whilst being at much higher risk of contracting the virus through daily interaction with the general public and they tend to be at the bottom end of retailers' salary scales.

A friend, the Liverpudlian comedian, author and historian John

Martin made many supportive and humorous posts during the lockdown, recognising the bravery of others, encouraging all to play their part and lifting spirits through comedy.

There are also three courageous and inspirational people from my hometown, who have continually helped me to keep a perspective on life, though their stories are very different.

Steve Prescott MBE

The late Steve Prescott made a massive contribution to one of my most enjoyable days out when his two tries in the Wembley sunshine helped St Helens beat Bradford Bulls in a classic Rugby League Challenge Cup final in 1996. However, that was just the start of his courageous and inspirational story.

Ten years on and Steve was diagnosed with pseudomyxoma peritonei, a rare and terminal form of cancer. He was absolutely determined to win his fight with cancer and succeeded when he underwent a pioneering multi-visceral transplant in 2013. Tragically, he succumbed to post-operative complications.

After the shock of his initial diagnosis, Steve set up the Steve Prescott Foundation and embarked on a series of incredible endurance events to raise money for Christies Cancer Hospital in Manchester and the RFL Benevolent Fund. Steve's initiative and leadership united the sport of Rugby League with players past and present supporting gruelling challenges including Marathons, the Three Peaks, Land's End to John O'Groats and events in the local community – all whilst under treatment for an incredibly debilitating disease. "The body achieves what the mind believes" became his motto and what he achieved physically was unbelievable.

Steve's courage and strength were there for all to see. On the inside, his drive was to show people that the cancer would not stop him living life to the full and inspire others to overcome adversity and meet challenges head on. He certainly had a major impact on me, and I cherish having a small part of his story, participating in some of the events and securing AG Barr's support.

Steve's wife Linzi completed his biography the year after he passed away and whilst he never showed it, to read about the physical agony he had to endure leaves you shaken yet bursting with admiration for how he coped. Steve and his family remain a hugely positive influence in St Helens and the Rugby League community. The Player of the Year in Super League is now aptly called The Steve Prescott Man of Steel Award. His Foundation continues a tradition of community events and fund-raising challenges supporting the charities and a research fund to study pseudomyxoma peritonei and related conditions. Steve Prescott was one in a million.

Andy Reid MBE

In 2009 Andy lost both of his legs and an arm serving his country in Afghanistan. After being flown back to the UK, Andy astounded people with his recovery by spending only two weeks in hospital being treated for his injuries before he was ready to make his first trip home. Since then he has become a successful local businessman and inspired others as a passionate Ambassador for the Soldiers Charity and other Amputees, helping raise funds and awareness. He has performed two tandem skydives, taken part in the Steve Prescott Foundation St Helen's 10K Run, abseiled down the Big One in Blackpool and countless other activities.

Andy is also an accomplished motivational speaker. His autobiography *'Standing Tall: The Inspirational Story of a True British Hero'* was published in 2013, and is a powerful read.

When I was a kid in the seventies, my favourite comic book was called Warlord. It glamorised the Second World War and featured a serious of ridiculous characters 'socking it to Jerry' and 'kicking Japanese butts'. After you have visited the War Cemeteries at Ypres and Normandy and met a true hero like Andy Reid, seeing him running a 10K on two prosthetic legs, it makes you embarrassed to have read such crap.

Damian Harper

Damian and I met when we started high school in 1980 and have been close friends ever since. He is a person of immense courage who I have held in utmost admiration for over thirty years.

When we were seventeen, Damian developed bone cancer in his left knee and had to have his whole leg amputated. On top of that he required intensive chemotherapy, and I can never forget visiting him in hospital and remembering how ill he was. As soon as he was able, he got back on with his life. Instead of returning to his A Levels he went to work for the NHS, passed his driving test and refused to let the loss of his leg prevent him from doing what most teenage boys want to do. He came out to the pub every week, chatted up girls, got drunk with the rest of us, hit the dance floor and still moved better than most. One evening a group of us went out for a drink and at last orders he was reluctant to go home. "I have some test results coming back tomorrow" he said, "and basically I'll find out if I'm going to live or die".

Over time he watched football and rugby league with 'the lads' and we had crazy nights out and weekends away. He progressed at work, studied for a degree, and bought a house with his partner Sue.

Unfortunately, there was little support or counselling for Damian in those days and in bravely getting on with life, it suppressed Post Traumatic Stress Disorder which surfaced in his forties with severe mental and emotional challenges. Life had cruelly knocked him again but with the support of Sue and digging deep into his reserves of determination he has battled demons and inspired others.

As a trustee of the Amputation Foundation he supports others affected like him and was part of an amputee group who climbed Kilimanjaro. He has made several TV appearances and featured in a BBC Four documentary No Body's Perfect culminating in a picture of Damian radiating power and confidence, taken by renowned photographer Rankin. Damian is an incredible human being and I'm very proud to be his friend.

We can understandably become anxious or stressed about jobs and careers, but before they can even consider their work aspirations, Damian and Andy have massive physical, mental and emotional challenges to overcome, that most cannot even begin to imagine.

It is unequivocally humbling to know people like Steve Prescott, Andy Reid, and Damian Harper. I hoped that if I ever had a serious setback like they've endured, I would be able to find a fraction of their courage.

No way, that couldn't happen to him!

I didn't plan to include this story initially. It just didn't feel right, as despite having a serious setback, unlike Andy and Damian I have been able to continue my career without major limitations. However, after meeting Nick Clarke from the charity Stroke Information, I'm hoping that sharing this experience may give hope and encouragement to others.

During 2015, and probably before that if I think back, I had what I described as a few 'funny turns' where I'd say sentences the wrong way round or mumble my words. I was prone to feeling a bit light-headed and having the odd headache which I'd just dismiss as fatigue or not having enough coffee. With a busy schedule, a responsible job and lots of travel, I didn't think much about it and just cracked on with things.

That summer at AG Barr had been hectic after the implementation of a huge operating systems project.

Our family holiday was on a well-earned break in Cornwall and one day as I sat on a deck chair relaxing, I tried to say something, but no words came out. I nodded off and thought it was just another funny turn. When we got home the following week, I went to the gym for a spin class, came home and made lunch.

I then went to my daughter's room to ask her to tidy up her holiday gear and when I went to speak, pure 'gobbledegook' came out for about 10 mins. I knew what I wanted to say but just made odd sounds. We both ended up laughing at my predicament and I resorted to sign language to tell her what I needed her to do.

I then had a strange feeling as if my head was floating all afternoon. I thought, "this isn't right" and booked in with my GP the next morning. I have a fabulous GP and she identified straight away that I may have had a transient ischaemic attack (TIA or mini-stroke). She asked my wife to take me straight to hospital.

I had various scans and tests, and it was bizarre to be pushed to a stroke ward in a wheelchair even though I could walk and function normally. After all the scans, a left lobal infarct was diagnosed. I'd not heard of an infarct before, but it means a small, localised area of dead tissue resulting from a blood supply failure. As often happens with TIAs a full ischaemic stroke had followed.

It all seemed quite surreal and like it wasn't happening. I was forty-six years old and 'fit as a fiddle'—how could this happen to me? There appeared to be no obvious reason for the stroke, though later tests revealed I had a significant hole in my heart. This isn't uncommon and many people go through their life totally oblivious to having one. However, if a blood clot gets through the hole, you are in trouble.

When we got home, I was exhausted. I got into bed thinking about what had happened and suddenly began sobbing uncontrollably. My mum had died suddenly of a brain haemorrhage when she was forty-seven and her mother had had multiple strokes in her old age. I think if anything, the tears were ones of relief that I was still here.

Fortunately, I was left with no real physical issues. My sense of balance isn't quite as good. I frequently bang into door frames and get fatigued but that's about it. I had the hole in my heart plugged with a PFO closure operation at Liverpool Heart and Chest Hospital in April 2016. It's a fascinating procedure that was performed under local anaesthetic so I could watch. I ran a marathon a year later with a better time than my first one. With a little titanium plug in my heart, I can joke that I'm now one per cent of being a terminator— one of my favourite series of films.

I probably went back to work too quickly. AG Barr was supportive, but I didn't want to fall behind or lose my self-confidence. I pushed myself to perform exactly as I had previously done and when you do that people tend to forget what you've been through. The stroke's impact on me is mostly hidden. It has resulted in fatigue, delayed memory recall and depression. These can be difficult to manage but they're nothing like the physical and mental challenges that Andy and Damian have to overcome. I count myself very lucky as it could have been so much worse. I look at the BBC journalist Andrew Marr, who has had a much tougher battle from a similar illness.

Strokes do not just affect older people and can have a devastating effect. If you ever experience loss of speech or have 'funny turns', don't ignore them; get checked out. There are thousands of worthy charities people can support, but please be aware of the terrible trauma that affects stroke survivors and the people close to them

REFLECTION

Catalysts

Culture eats strategy for breakfast - *Peter Drucker.*

When I joined Procter and Gamble in 1990, I expected I would work there until I retired. It was a marvellous blue-chip company with a real focus on developing its people. Richard Dupree, the post-war CEO, famously declared, "If you leave us our money, our buildings and our brands, but take away our people, the Company will fail. But if you take away our money, our buildings and our brands, but leave us our people, we can rebuild the whole thing in a decade". The formative years of my career were very much in a business that reflected Drucker's views.

In a way, I left Kellogg's because although it had many similarities with Procter & Gamble, it just wasn't the same, particularly in the areas of leadership and commitment to its people.

At AG Barr, for the first ten years or so, I had the autonomy to use my experience and principles to build the type of team environment that I had aspired to. We delivered fantastic results and comments from colleagues confirmed how much they enjoyed the environment.

Towards the end of my time at Barr, I knew that as an individual I was becoming somewhat stale, and the company's results and culture were changing. From my perspective, we were heading in the opposite direction to Drucker's quote so when a conversation began about a restructure including my departure, it was unexpected, but ultimately quite welcomed.

After leaving AG Barr in the summer of 2019, 1 accepted a position as the chief commercial officer at Flavour Warehouse, a business specialising in smoking cessation (e-liquids and vaping), not a category I was ever going to become a consumer of. As a passionate anti-smoker, I considered vaping a less harmful alternative for the vaper and especially third-party bystanders.

It was a fascinating change to be part of a successful, ambitious SME business and there was a lot about the role I enjoyed. There were multiple challenges across my remit of sales and marketing and some gaps in personnel to fit the structure I had proposed. A few things troubled me, like a lack of trust and transparency across the organisation, but I remained philosophical and considered that change in such areas would need to be influenced gradually.

I was quite surprised when my time at Flavour Warehouse was cut short. I had worked really hard and was making a positive impact, but my services were suddenly no longer required without being given any real explanation.

Maybe I had been working for Uncle Joe? Certainly, there wasn't much conviction for Drucker's beliefs. The net result was a need for some alchemy to turn my situation around. After a brief period of reflection, then the enforced inactivity of the first lockdown, the recipe for *Baked Alaska* began to form. I had thought about it for years, so it was now or never

Self-Reflection

Someone reading this may think, 'Okay wise guy, it's all very well to highlight the mistakes of others, but are you really qualified to comment?' Many of my peers, others I worked with and some who worked for me, are now MDs and CEOs of some significant businesses,

So it would be a fair question. I have thought about this a lot and I believe the answers come down to three factors: Style (KSA), Circumstances and Comparison.

Style

With good A-levels and an upper second degree in Business Studies, the intelligence is there. What I have lacked in the ***knowledge*** area had probably been due to switching off from work related subjects. I found 'talking shop' quite boring and tend to socialise less with work colleagues. When younger I worried about being judged if I had a few too many drinks and showed drunken antics as I would with my close friends.

I have never been one for leaving a training course and getting stuck into all the follow-up reading. Some articles and commentaries have had a tangible impact over the years, and I have usually participated wholeheartedly in training programs on the day. However, as an example, whilst GAP Partnership's training on negotiation is excellent, I have never been motivated enough to plough through every page of their accompanying book, *The 48 Laws of Power*.

I am very grateful for the support from my employers in developing my ***skills***. As individuals, we all map out differently and I'd point to a strong track record in developing people and successful, productive relationships with customers. In the corporate world I have been less enthusiastic about the internal and analytical projects that tend to get you noticed by the highest-ranking officers. I have also been outspoken, having witnessed the damage caused by the Emperor's New Clothes. This is possibly the key reason that many of my peers have gone on to secure bigger and more influential roles. I commend and congratulate them for finding the right blend.

The final consideration is ***attitude***—desire, behaviours, and hunger for success. I've had a successful career; however, I've sometimes lacked self-confidence, been resistant to change and probably been dogged by self-doubt and impostor syndrome. When I don't really know something or lack expertise in an area, it shows. I have seen others who carry this challenge with far greater aplomb. I was told early in my career that I was too open and honest ('wears his heart on his sleeve') and hence unlikely to make it beyond sales director—words that proved quite prophetic.

The legendary Dundee United Football Club manager Jim McClean used to stand on the touchline at training, screaming with frustration at the young, well-paid players coming through. He would bellow that 'they didn't want it' as much as he did.

Circumstances

As described earlier, after starting in a great company where I could learn and develop, I probably ended up in the wrong environments for me to thrive, where there was less emphasis on leadership and culture and more focus on projects and analysis.

Maybe my style and qualities have just not been fully appreciated in environments where my skill set became less valued. However, As Bob Dylan once sang, "the times they are a changin" and the likes of Patrick Lencioni and Simon Sinek herald a new era where success is based on trust, transparency, vulnerability and appreciation of others. *The way I have always operated and encouraged.*

Whilst the Gospel of Matthew may have been written over two thousand years ago, it seems that now in business the 'salt of the earth' types are becoming much more appreciated and can lead organisations to great success.

Comparisons

An interesting article in GQ *Magazine* by Jacqueline Hurst caught my eye in which she describes 'comparison as the thief of joy', going on to say that comparison is a waste of your time. Many of us commence our careers with specific aspirations, but over time I believe Maslow's model still holds true and once lower order needs have been met, esteem needs and self-actualisation needs differ massively as we are all unique. As Jacqueline says, "Someone else's intelligence / body / financial status does not mean they are better than you." The messages of gratitude and goodwill I received on leaving AG Barr meant far more to me than if I'd been given a better bonus that year. They are comments I will cherish for a long time and provide reassurance that in the most part I have done right by others. And that is coming from someone who, as a shallow twenty- one-year-old used a graduation loan on a second-hand Rolex!

Comparison can be constructive if it's used as a benchmark to help you improve. Certainly, measuring your knowledge and skills against successful, more experienced operators can help significantly, though we've covered the danger of mimicking others' attitudes and behaviours and trying to be someone you're not.

Real Life Benchmark

Whilst searching through files and memorabilia for writing this book, I came across a card that a friend sent to me when my mother died unexpectedly during my second year at university. It was a very kind and considerate action that brought great comfort at the time. We had lived near to each other but had attended different schools, though we both studied for A-levels at the same sixth form college and rode the bus together every day. We eventually lost touch, and I never knew until a few years ago that we had both followed careers in the grocery industry, myself on the supply side and Joanne in accountancy, before entering retail.

The Joanne referred to is Jo Whitfield, the CEO of Co-operative Food. I am delighted with Jo's success. To become the first female CEO of one of the big UK food retailers is a landmark achievement. Jo's kindness, consideration and decency are combined with an acute business brain. She is leading Co-operative to outstanding results and playing a vital role in our communities, particularly during the

Covid-19 crisis. Jo is a fantastic example of a phenomenal business leader who has made it all the way and is most definitely 'salt of the earth'. She grew up a few houses away from Steve Prescott-such inspiration from one small street in St Helens!

A source of Pride

The comedian Johnny Vegas and singer Jacqui Abbott of the Beautiful South are also from nearby. Our neighbours in Liverpool have long had a reputation for producing entertainers and they are never shy in letting the world know about it. St Helens is a much, much smaller town but is also a great source of talent on several fronts in the arts, sport and business.

Our town's original crest bears the Latin inscription *ex terra lucem* or 'light out of the earth'. As the post Covid-19 society continues to change around us, hopefully more and more people will realise that recognising and championing salt of the earth qualities can elevate us all to a higher plane.

MY NEW MISSION: BACK TO THE FUTURE

My new mission is going back to the future as a Business Doctor in my local area, to support and share my experience with businesses. I want to help them grow, achieve their vision and develop the wider economy in northwest England.

A huge amount was invested in my training and development by the companies I've worked for and I enjoy passing on the learning from these powerful and transformational programmes, that may otherwise be beyond the resources of a typical SME. I am also sharing my experience by facilitating training through St Helens Chamber and have received the appropriate accreditation to work in schools and colleges, which I will really enjoy.

We have clear structure and processes to work with as Business Doctors and a variety of effective tools to deploy within our clients' businesses. We have vast experience at our disposal and we have so far supported over ten thousand businesses in the UK. We provide affordable support to help business owners make the right choices for growth. Practice, dedication and experience have made us experts in our field, but what particularly attracted me to Business Doctors was their down-to-earth approach. We don't just coach; we get on the pitch.

For me though, it still comes down to those two key building blocks from my Procter & Gamble days: *Leading people and building business.*

What I always enjoyed and what helped to keep me motivated through my sales and marketing career was the variety in my responsibilities. Selling, planning, negotiation, analysis, coaching, training, recruiting— mine was never a nine-to-five or desk-bound role. However, around forty thousand miles of driving, twenty to twenty-five long train journeys and a dozen or so flights every year did take its toll and one benefit of Covid-19 is the emergence of

Zoom, Teams and so on as viable alternatives to some of that travel!

Back to Business Doctors and that variety of responsibilities and different challenges is still very much there and, if anything, is even greater.

In closing, I'd like to say good luck to all my readers in your careers and with your business ventures. I hope by reading this you have gained some simple ideas and suggestions for supporting your personal development and enhancing your leadership, based on the successes and mistakes of myself and others. I also hope that some of the stories shared have raised a smile, as we all need a bit of levity in our lives.

PICTURES SAY A THOUSAND WORDS

Early Days

I never met my maternal grandfather Evander Jackson Tames as he died before I was born. He was an interesting character who became bitter and resentful of the society and leaders who had taken the country into the appalling carnage of World War One. He was a confirmed atheist and associate of the renowned socialist and future Labour MP for Liverpool Exchange, Bessie Braddock. They were both involved in the Liverpool branch of the Communist Party of Great Britain in the 1920's. I have a few of my grandfather's possessions including a First Edition Printing of Erich Maria Remarque's classic anti-war novel All Quiet on the Western Front and his Air Raid Warden Whistle from the Second World War. I also have a little booklet belonging to my mother in which he wrote some very important and enduring advice when she was just nine years old in 1951 – "Actions speak louder than words"

His actions certainly spoke louder than his words. He walked the talk by not actually walking, as being an atheist, he would not go into church for my mother and father's wedding, only joining them later for the reception!

My first real leadership role was captaining my Primary School football team. I am holding the ball and you can see that we won a few trophies.

St Helen's town crest. From the earth comes light.

University of Sheffield 1987-90

With my mum the morning I departed for the University of Sheffield. Unfortunately, she never got to see me graduate.

Despite suddenly losing my mum in my second year, I loved being at Sheffield University and was elected President of Sorby Hall of Residence Junior Common Room. Each year we had a hall photograph taken. It was the old style, slow exposure panoramic photo and if quick enough, someone could start on the left, run around the back and appear again on the right-hand side! On the second of the three sections from 1988 is a future European Zone President of Anheuser-Busch InBev and at the time of writing the current MD of Weetabix.

The outgoing Hall President Joe McCarthy is sat central next to the Hall Warden and I'm over on the right in the final section below, about twelve in on the third row up.

Below is a photo of Joe and I at the Formal Dinner to hand over the Presidency. In some ways we had little in common but became good friends. Joe was a great support when I lost my mum and pushed me really hard to pass my exams and learn from his own experience of having to re-sit exams over the previous summer.

He was an amazing character and would surely have achieved incredible things in his life, if it had not been cruelly brought short through the Hillsborough Tragedy. You'll Never Walk Alone Joe.

Procter & Gamble 1990-99

It was holding student office that brought me to the attention of Procter & Gamble, and they invited me to attend their Sales Management Vacation Course at the end of 1989. It ran for three days at the Runnymede Hotel in Surrey and was the first time I had ever stayed in a hotel. I am central on the back row. Sales VP John Millen occupies the central position. He was a true gentleman and a great leader who offered me the chance to return to P&G if my move to Kellogg's did not work out.

Note they were still using the Moon and Thirteen Stars Symbol – if there were any satanic orgies I wasn't invited. I returned as a trainer on the course several years later.

I was offered a job as Account Executive in Sales, providing I passed my degree. £13,400 a year with a company car too. How could I resist!

My Dad worked as a forklift truck driver on a three-shift system at Ford's Halewood car factory for over thirty years. The workforce in the seventies and eighties were really militant and it sometimes seemed like they were on strike more than they worked. Our parents wanted much better for their children. I worked as a summer intern at the plant in 1989. The picture below is from a 30 year service celebratory lunch for my Dad (right hand side)

Training at Procter & Gamble was first class. Two courses in one month!

I was invited to return to Sheffield University for a week, as a Young Manager helping undergraduates on a Career Development course (fourth from left)

At my desk in Procter & Gamble's Harrogate Office 1994, looking a bit worse for wear. Check out the size of that Monitor and Desk Top Computer!

I did not really enjoy my time in Head Office in Gosforth. The role was great experience, and I worked with some very talented people, but it was a bit too formal for me. Judge for yourself from the management meeting photo below, November 1995, only Ricky Reed looks happy!

After Gosforth, I moved to Procter & Gamble's Health & Beauty Care Division where the culture was a lot more relaxed. This was a team building event at a sales meeting I'm at the back second right.

My Asda ABCD Award. They may well have become more of a gimmick over time however, this is an authentic early edition signed by Allan Leighton CEO and sent direct to John Millen, Procter & Gamble's sales vice president. I've kept it for over twenty years and am proud of it!

AWARD

"Above and Beyond the Call of Duty"

This certifies that

Steve Smith

has received this award for actions truly Above and Beyond the Call of Duty.

ALLAN LEIGHTON
Chief Executive

My first real team – the Wild Geese of Skelmersdale. The UK General Manager, Mohan Mohan had heard good things about the culture we'd developed and paid a visit. His replacement 'talked the talk' but did not walk it from my experience. Margaret next to me was originally the team PA. We developed her role into an Office Manager. Second from left is Greg Jackson the founder and CEO of Octopus Energy.

A European Sales College Training course in 1998 where I was a moderator (back row second left) supporting the course leader (first left) Kevin Hawkins. Kevin was my manager for my National Account role on Kwik Save and had a discerning taste in dessert!

I really enjoyed the European Training, meeting colleagues from various countries. This was still relatively soon after the fall of the Berlin Wall and the opening up of Eastern Europe's economies.

Kellogg's 1999-04

Dinner (tea) one evening on my first Kellogg's sales and marketing conference in January 2000 in Puerto Banus. As part of the leadership group, I was in Spain for nearly a week. The previous year, the conference had been at Slaley Hall, Northumberland. It was dark, cold and rained incessantly. The new MD who'd just joined from Australia was horrified. 'F**k that, we're goin' somewhere sunny next year!' was his frequently repeated quote.

The England 1966 World Cup Winners in 2002, with myself next to the late, great Alan Ball on the right. We had TV and press coverage lined up to promote Kellogg's involvement until Roy Keane intervened! Still, a great night was had by all. Alan, June from the Co-op and myself were the last ones standing in the hotel afterwards. I helped Alan back to his room about 4am! One of my most enjoyable career evenings!

The free toys in boxes of cereal were a key part of growing up in the seventies and eighties, though the comparison with the more expensive toys McDonalds provided with Happy Meals was a significant challenge.

I had loads of fun working with Kellogg's Kids brands, providing fact filled Growth Charts and free "foot-bowls" with in-store purchase. This execution continued long after I had departed and there must still be thousands in kitchen cupboards across the UK. For one project Variety Pack packaging became trucks, buses and even Santa's Sleigh. Another promotion delivered a Free T-Shirt. Kellogg's also supported some fabulous movie launches through partnerships with Disney and Warner Brothers.

AG Barr 2004-19

R & R's more typical meaning as we launched Rockstar in 2007. Sir Anwar Pervez, Chairman of Bestway Group is central. We gave customers a real taste of Las Vegas with a helicopter trip to the Grand Canyon and ringside seats for the Rocky Hatton / Floyd Mayweather fight.

Ringside with Lennox Lewis. I also shook hands with Brad Pitt—Angelina Jolie looking on, somewhat bemused. To be fair, a day at work doesn't really get much better than this.

Las Vegas 2016. I am third from right, Martin Race then Bestway's MD is third from left.

Presenting Rockstar to customers in Glasgow, looking cool!

Talking football with Everton manager David Moyes at the Scottish Football League Awards in 2010. It was fascinating to hear about the inner workings of football and discuss the importance of IRN-BRU in Scotland.

Barr participated in several Charity Celebrity Football Tournaments organised by key grocery retailers. Great fun, a good chance to get to know senior figures in the customers and an opportunity to test yourself against ex Pros. We got to the final one year, but never quite got our hands on a trophy.

We had a very close relationship with the Prince and Princess of Wales Hospice in Glasgow. As well as accepting one of their charity places for the 2008 London Marathon (I raised four thousand, five hundred pounds with some very generous donations, particularly from customers) the team raised thousands for the hospice's 'Brick by Brick' appeal to help fund the move to new premises. Each year we sponsored the hospice's main fundraising event, the Sportsman's Dinner.

In the picture above are Jan Molby (former Liverpool footballer), Sean Styles (comedian), Fergus Slattery and Martin Bayfield (Ireland/ England and Lions rugby union internationals respectively). On other occasions I got to meet my own childhood football heroes Duncan McKenzie and Johan Cruyff, Manchester United stars Gary Neville and Peter Schmeichel, boxing legend Joe Calzaghe and tennis ace Greg Rusedski—plus many others. An absolute privilege to be on the top table with such achievers.

When IRN-BRU invested in becoming Official Soft Drink of Super League we were determined to get really involved with the sport and not just be a passive sponsor. We held our Sales Meetings at Rugby League stadiums such as St Helens, Wigan and at Warrington pictured in 2011.

To help the sales team relate to the sport, I invited the late Steve Prescott MBE (front centre with grey jacket flanked by myself and Roger the CEO) to share his story about success on the field and then fighting stomach cancer off it. His incredible endurance feats during fund raising challenges, whilst battling the debilitating disease were an inspiration. This was one of his first public speaking engagements and he admitted to a fair degree of nerves. He was asked about this by one of the audience who wondered how he could perform so well in front of 100,000 people in a Challenge Cup Final at Wembley yet be nervous talking in front of our group. Steve's answer illustrates the power of teamwork and interdependency – "I had twelve mates on the pitch supporting me at Wembley, here I'm on my own".

We were proud to support the Steve Prescott Foundation in fundraising events. I am partnering Premier League referee Chris Foy in the dragon boat race, with Steve behind me.

With my son and guests on the pitch at St Helen's Rugby League Club after sponsoring a game.

One of the few high points of 2020 was when the Saints edged out fierce rivals Wigan at the end of the Super League Grand Final. The word 'derby' to describe sports events between near neighbours originated from this fixture.

These historical combatants fought out a truly titanic struggle, only decided by the last play of the game. No one deserved to lose and despite my St Helens' allegiance I did genuinely feel for Wigan and their supporters.

What also stood out was the humility and sportsmanship of the Wigan captain Sean O'Loughlin. In the final game of a long and illustrious career, his grace and magnanimity in defeat was something you rarely see in other sports.

Celebrating two of our successes in the Bestway Awards, firstly with Guy and Vinnie in 2012 – they did an incredible job developing our relevance and relationship with one of the UK's largest wholesalers. I always insisted that Vinnie or Guy receive the award, they were the ones who earned them.

We won again in 2013. Guy and Vinnie are joined by Steve Brooks (second left, who ran the Regional Sales Team) Steven, Deryn and Stevie. They had over 100 years AG Barr service between them and created a new form of artwork by building incredible displays in UK Cash & Carries.

Below is the Dubai Palm, re-created in Rubicon Juice and KA.

Presenting to AG Barr's Middlebrook Office, near Bolton.

A great place to work, full of life, with wonderful friendly colleagues and described by one person as a 'sanctuary'. We obtained Investors In People (IIP) Silver Status and always got the highest site scores in AG Barr's Employee Engagement Survey.

Karen is front row central and was a great support. Her role developed from Sales Secretarial Supervisor up to Office Manager, leading the team sat on the front row.

Michelle from the operations team later replied to one of my posts on LinkedIn, writing: 'You are an inspiration. Your kind, encouraging and positive attitude and behaviour will stay with me. You touched peoples' lives and I don't think you know what a lasting impression you made.'

To have someone who did not even report to you summarise your career with such words is simply priceless.

There were some great characters but the quiet, library like atmosphere at Barr Head Office had a somnambulant effect. We were always encouraged to 'let our hair down' and have fun at the Annual Company Conference though! Over the years I presented dressed as a Spartan Hoplite, Spitfire Pilot, Adam Ant and wearing Bavarian Lederhosen.

The last meeting with my AG Barr team. Jonathan the Commercial Director is sat next to me and "Wee Ian" behind. Ian led the team in Scotland to multiple SWA Awards and was one of the great characters I met during my career. Relevance and Relationship were really strong 'north of the border'.

The Café on the Pier at Lytham St Annes gave us exclusive use of their facilities for and looked after us only too well! Bad heads the next day.

AG Barr plc Share Price performance during the time I was there. I left in July 2019. The price dropped significantly. I am 'just saying... there was probably more to it than that!

ACKNOWLEDGEMENTS

I have worked with so many people over the course of my career that I have chosen to just pick out a few key names who had a positive impact. There are many, many others who I have looked at with respect and followed their example, then also those whose modus operandi I have questioned and decided to handle situations in what I considered a better way. Either way, major learnings were taken from both and I am grateful. There are also many incredibly gifted people I've referenced who can explain their work far better.

At the University of Sheffield, I enjoyed the marketing lectures by Everett M Jacobs and in later life fully appreciated the lessons in maturity provided by Dr David E Bland OBE. I have also never forgotten Anthony Levi. If he hadn't driven a Ford Transit Minibus over the A57 Snake Pass in the early hours of a wet January morning, I'd never have seen my mum before she died. I am eternally grateful to Anthony.

Joining Procter & Gamble was crucial to how I developed. I was recruited by Steve Gray, and then Kevin C Hawkins supplied excellent guidance and the idea behind this story a long time ago. John Forsyth showed a willingness to think differently and challenge the status quo, whilst Richard C H Reed is a quintessential English gentleman who cared for his people and finds time, even now, to provide help and support.

At Kellogg's, Stephen Twaddell recruited me to be part of his crusade to modernise the sales function. The training he commissioned has helped me ever since by introducing the inspirational thinking of Helen-Jane Nelson of Cecara Consulting. Dan Beck reported to me in Kellogg's and eventually followed me to AG Barr where he provided friendship, support, and the benefit of his unique skillset.

I spent fifteen years with AG Barr working directly for commercial director Jonathan D Kemp, one of the brightest people I ever worked with. He was previously my friend at Procter & Gamble (despite inheriting the MBW project from me!). We made a great partnership, with a complimentary blend of the 3E's. Finance director Stuart Lorimer shared kind and encouraging words when I was leaving. Karen Sharpies, originally my PA and then promoted to office manager was an absolute pleasure to work with and a key confidante. Karen's team were great fun, and we had some hilarious moments in the Middlebrook office.

Others who have provided support in various ways include Kevin and Rosemary Taylor from Vivvid, Martin Race, former MD of Bestway, Miles Mandelson my next-door neighbour and Matt Keeffe who provided valuable feedback on early versions. Bill Byrne the MD of Churchill Search & Selection has been a great friend and sounding board for twenty-five years with Matt Levington, Rod Davies and Kevin 'Obi-wan' Cook of Business Doctors now fulfilling that role. Andrew Selley, CEO of Bidcorp, is a leader who impressed me greatly in his role as chairman of the Federation of Wholesale Distributors. Andrew introduced me to the wonderful Denise Roberts of The Editor's Chair who made Baked Alaska become a reality.

Alan McKie of Halton Chamber has offered me loads of encouragement, whilst John Tabern, CEO of The Standing Tall Foundation and chairman of St Helens Town Deal Board is someone I've worked with on various projects over the years. I've been warmly welcomed into the local business community and appreciate the help given by the likes of Lisa McAllister, Jayne Shufflebotham, Geoff Bates' team at St Helens Chamber and Jim Toohey who I first met over thirty years ago when he was a store manager with Morrisons.

Colin Parry OBE is someone I have admired from afar for a long, long time and it was a pleasure meeting him in 2019 for coaching and support.

To me, he defines the word dignity. It was a genuine honour when he agreed to write a foreword.

Last, but certainly not least, is my wife Gillian who nursed me through my stroke recovery and has always had more confidence in my abilities than I have had myself. I would never have completed this without her love, positivity, and encouragement